C-4208 CAREER EXAMINATION SERIES

This is your
PASSBOOK for...

Private Patrol Operator

Test Preparation Study Guide
Questions & Answers

COPYRIGHT NOTICE

This book is SOLELY intended for, is sold ONLY to, and its use is RESTRICTED to individual, bona fide applicants or candidates who qualify by virtue of having seriously filed applications for appropriate license, certificate, professional and/or promotional advancement, higher school matriculation, scholarship, or other legitimate requirements of education and/or governmental authorities.

This book is NOT intended for use, class instruction, tutoring, training, duplication, copying, reprinting, excerption, or adaptation, etc., by:

1) Other publishers
2) Proprietors and/or Instructors of "Coaching" and/or Preparatory Courses
3) Personnel and/or Training Divisions of commercial, industrial, and governmental organizations
4) Schools, colleges, or universities and/or their departments and staffs, including teachers and other personnel
5) Testing Agencies or Bureaus
6) Study groups which seek by the purchase of a single volume to copy and/or duplicate and/or adapt this material for use by the group as a whole without having purchased individual volumes for each of the members of the group
7) Et al.

Such persons would be in violation of appropriate Federal and State statutes.

PROVISION OF LICENSING AGREEMENTS – Recognized educational, commercial, industrial, and governmental institutions and organizations, and others legitimately engaged in educational pursuits, including training, testing, and measurement activities, may address request for a licensing agreement to the copyright owners, who will determine whether, and under what conditions, including fees and charges, the materials in this book may be used them. In other words, a licensing facility exists for the legitimate use of the material in this book on other than an individual basis. However, it is asseverated and affirmed here that the material in this book CANNOT be used without the receipt of the express permission of such a licensing agreement from the Publishers. Inquiries re licensing should be addressed to the company, attention rights and permissions department.

All rights reserved, including the right of reproduction in whole or in part, in any form or by any means, electronic or mechanical, including photocopying, recording, or by any information storage and retrieval system, without permission in writing from the Publisher.

Copyright © 2024 by
National Learning Corporation

212 Michael Drive, Syosset, NY 11791
(516) 921-8888 • www.passbooks.com
E-mail: info@passbooks.com

PUBLISHED IN THE UNITED STATES OF AMERICA

PASSBOOK® SERIES

THE *PASSBOOK® SERIES* has been created to prepare applicants and candidates for the ultimate academic battlefield – the examination room.

At some time in our lives, each and every one of us may be required to take an examination – for validation, matriculation, admission, qualification, registration, certification, or licensure.

Based on the assumption that every applicant or candidate has met the basic formal educational standards, has taken the required number of courses, and read the necessary texts, the *PASSBOOK® SERIES* furnishes the one special preparation which may assure passing with confidence, instead of failing with insecurity. Examination questions – together with answers – are furnished as the basic vehicle for study so that the mysteries of the examination and its compounding difficulties may be eliminated or diminished by a sure method.

This book is meant to help you pass your examination provided that you qualify and are serious in your objective.

The entire field is reviewed through the huge store of content information which is succinctly presented through a provocative and challenging approach – the question-and-answer method.

A climate of success is established by furnishing the correct answers at the end of each test.

You soon learn to recognize types of questions, forms of questions, and patterns of questioning. You may even begin to anticipate expected outcomes.

You perceive that many questions are repeated or adapted so that you can gain acute insights, which may enable you to score many sure points.

You learn how to confront new questions, or types of questions, and to attack them confidently and work out the correct answers.

You note objectives and emphases, and recognize pitfalls and dangers, so that you may make positive educational adjustments.

Moreover, you are kept fully informed in relation to new concepts, methods, practices, and directions in the field.

You discover that you are actually taking the examination all the time: you are preparing for the examination by "taking" an examination, not by reading extraneous and/or supererogatory textbooks.

In short, this PASSBOOK®, used directedly, should be an important factor in helping you to pass your test.

PRIVATE PATROL OPERATOR

A Private Patrol Operator operates a business that protects persons or property or prevents theft. In order for a person or a company to seek licensure as a Private Patrol Operator, the applicant must have passed the licensing examination. An individual, partnership, or corporation seeking a license as a Private Patrol Operator must specify in the application the individual who will manage the business on a day-to-day basis. This individual is called the Qualified Manager. You may not carry a gun on duty without a valid firearm permit. You may not carry a concealed weapon on duty without a concealed weapons permit issued by local authorities, nor carry a caliber handgun not listed on your firearm permit.

SUBJECT OF EXAMINATION

The multiple choice examination will cover security service rules and regulations, business knowledge, emergency procedures, security functions, use of deadly weapons and other related areas.

HOW TO TAKE A TEST

I. YOU MUST PASS AN EXAMINATION

A. WHAT EVERY CANDIDATE SHOULD KNOW

Examination applicants often ask us for help in preparing for the written test. What can I study in advance? What kinds of questions will be asked? How will the test be given? How will the papers be graded?

As an applicant for a civil service examination, you may be wondering about some of these things. Our purpose here is to suggest effective methods of advance study and to describe civil service examinations.

Your chances for success on this examination can be increased if you know how to prepare. Those "pre-examination jitters" can be reduced if you know what to expect. You can even experience an adventure in good citizenship if you know why civil service exams are given.

B. WHY ARE CIVIL SERVICE EXAMINATIONS GIVEN?

Civil service examinations are important to you in two ways. As a citizen, you want public jobs filled by employees who know how to do their work. As a job seeker, you want a fair chance to compete for that job on an equal footing with other candidates. The best-known means of accomplishing this two-fold goal is the competitive examination.

Exams are widely publicized throughout the nation. They may be administered for jobs in federal, state, city, municipal, town or village governments or agencies.

Any citizen may apply, with some limitations, such as the age or residence of applicants. Your experience and education may be reviewed to see whether you meet the requirements for the particular examination. When these requirements exist, they are reasonable and applied consistently to all applicants. Thus, a competitive examination may cause you some uneasiness now, but it is your privilege and safeguard.

C. HOW ARE CIVIL SERVICE EXAMS DEVELOPED?

Examinations are carefully written by trained technicians who are specialists in the field known as "psychological measurement," in consultation with recognized authorities in the field of work that the test will cover. These experts recommend the subject matter areas or skills to be tested; only those knowledges or skills important to your success on the job are included. The most reliable books and source materials available are used as references. Together, the experts and technicians judge the difficulty level of the questions.

Test technicians know how to phrase questions so that the problem is clearly stated. Their ethics do not permit "trick" or "catch" questions. Questions may have been tried out on sample groups, or subjected to statistical analysis, to determine their usefulness.

Written tests are often used in combination with performance tests, ratings of training and experience, and oral interviews. All of these measures combine to form the best-known means of finding the right person for the right job.

II. HOW TO PASS THE WRITTEN TEST

A. NATURE OF THE EXAMINATION

To prepare intelligently for civil service examinations, you should know how they differ from school examinations you have taken. In school you were assigned certain definite pages to read or subjects to cover. The examination questions were quite detailed and usually emphasized memory. Civil service exams, on the other hand, try to discover your present ability to perform the duties of a position, plus your potentiality to learn these duties. In other words, a civil service exam attempts to predict how successful you will be. Questions cover such a broad area that they cannot be as minute and detailed as school exam questions.

In the public service similar kinds of work, or positions, are grouped together in one "class." This process is known as *position-classification*. All the positions in a class are paid according to the salary range for that class. One class title covers all of these positions, and they are all tested by the same examination.

B. FOUR BASIC STEPS

1) Study the announcement

How, then, can you know what subjects to study? Our best answer is: "Learn as much as possible about the class of positions for which you've applied." The exam will test the knowledge, skills and abilities needed to do the work.

Your most valuable source of information about the position you want is the official exam announcement. This announcement lists the training and experience qualifications. Check these standards and apply only if you come reasonably close to meeting them.

The brief description of the position in the examination announcement offers some clues to the subjects which will be tested. Think about the job itself. Review the duties in your mind. Can you perform them, or are there some in which you are rusty? Fill in the blank spots in your preparation.

Many jurisdictions preview the written test in the exam announcement by including a section called "Knowledge and Abilities Required," "Scope of the Examination," or some similar heading. Here you will find out specifically what fields will be tested.

2) Review your own background

Once you learn in general what the position is all about, and what you need to know to do the work, ask yourself which subjects you already know fairly well and which need improvement. You may wonder whether to concentrate on improving your strong areas or on building some background in your fields of weakness. When the announcement has specified "some knowledge" or "considerable knowledge," or has used adjectives like "beginning principles of…" or "advanced … methods," you can get a clue as to the number and difficulty of questions to be asked in any given field. More questions, and hence broader coverage, would be included for those subjects which are more important in the work. Now weigh your strengths and weaknesses against the job requirements and prepare accordingly.

3) Determine the level of the position

Another way to tell how intensively you should prepare is to understand the level of the job for which you are applying. Is it the entering level? In other words, is this the position in which beginners in a field of work are hired? Or is it an intermediate or advanced level? Sometimes this is indicated by such words as "Junior" or "Senior" in the class title. Other jurisdictions use Roman numerals to designate the level – Clerk I, Clerk II, for example. The word "Supervisor" sometimes appears in the title. If the level is not indicated by the title, check the description of duties. Will you be working under very close supervision, or will you have responsibility for independent decisions in this work?

4) Choose appropriate study materials

Now that you know the subjects to be examined and the relative amount of each subject to be covered, you can choose suitable study materials. For beginning level jobs, or even advanced ones, if you have a pronounced weakness in some aspect of your training, read a modern, standard textbook in that field. Be sure it is up to date and has general coverage. Such books are normally available at your library, and the librarian will be glad to help you locate one. For entry-level positions, questions of appropriate difficulty are chosen – neither highly advanced questions, nor those too simple. Such questions require careful thought but not advanced training.

If the position for which you are applying is technical or advanced, you will read more advanced, specialized material. If you are already familiar with the basic principles of your field, elementary textbooks would waste your time. Concentrate on advanced textbooks and technical periodicals. Think through the concepts and review difficult problems in your field.

These are all general sources. You can get more ideas on your own initiative, following these leads. For example, training manuals and publications of the government agency which employs workers in your field can be useful, particularly for technical and professional positions. A letter or visit to the government department involved may result in more specific study suggestions, and certainly will provide you with a more definite idea of the exact nature of the position you are seeking.

III. KINDS OF TESTS

Tests are used for purposes other than measuring knowledge and ability to perform specified duties. For some positions, it is equally important to test ability to make adjustments to new situations or to profit from training. In others, basic mental abilities not dependent on information are essential. Questions which test these things may not appear as pertinent to the duties of the position as those which test for knowledge and information. Yet they are often highly important parts of a fair examination. For very general questions, it is almost impossible to help you direct your study efforts. What we can do is to point out some of the more common of these general abilities needed in public service positions and describe some typical questions.

1) General information

Broad, general information has been found useful for predicting job success in some kinds of work. This is tested in a variety of ways, from vocabulary lists to questions about current events. Basic background in some field of work, such as sociology or economics, may be sampled in a group of questions. Often these are principles which have become familiar to most persons through exposure rather than through formal training. It is difficult to advise you how to study for these questions; being alert to the world around you is our best suggestion.

2) Verbal ability

An example of an ability needed in many positions is verbal or language ability. Verbal ability is, in brief, the ability to use and understand words. Vocabulary and grammar tests are typical measures of this ability. Reading comprehension or paragraph interpretation questions are common in many kinds of civil service tests. You are given a paragraph of written material and asked to find its central meaning.

3) Numerical ability
Number skills can be tested by the familiar arithmetic problem, by checking paired lists of numbers to see which are alike and which are different, or by interpreting charts and graphs. In the latter test, a graph may be printed in the test booklet which you are asked to use as the basis for answering questions.

4) Observation
A popular test for law-enforcement positions is the observation test. A picture is shown to you for several minutes, then taken away. Questions about the picture test your ability to observe both details and larger elements.

5) Following directions
In many positions in the public service, the employee must be able to carry out written instructions dependably and accurately. You may be given a chart with several columns, each column listing a variety of information. The questions require you to carry out directions involving the information given in the chart.

6) Skills and aptitudes
Performance tests effectively measure some manual skills and aptitudes. When the skill is one in which you are trained, such as typing or shorthand, you can practice. These tests are often very much like those given in business school or high school courses. For many of the other skills and aptitudes, however, no short-time preparation can be made. Skills and abilities natural to you or that you have developed throughout your lifetime are being tested.

Many of the general questions just described provide all the data needed to answer the questions and ask you to use your reasoning ability to find the answers. Your best preparation for these tests, as well as for tests of facts and ideas, is to be at your physical and mental best. You, no doubt, have your own methods of getting into an exam-taking mood and keeping "in shape." The next section lists some ideas on this subject.

IV. KINDS OF QUESTIONS

Only rarely is the "essay" question, which you answer in narrative form, used in civil service tests. Civil service tests are usually of the short-answer type. Full instructions for answering these questions will be given to you at the examination. But in case this is your first experience with short-answer questions and separate answer sheets, here is what you need to know:

1) Multiple-choice Questions
Most popular of the short-answer questions is the "multiple choice" or "best answer" question. It can be used, for example, to test for factual knowledge, ability to solve problems or judgment in meeting situations found at work.
A multiple-choice question is normally one of three types—
- It can begin with an incomplete statement followed by several possible endings. You are to find the one ending which *best* completes the statement, although some of the others may not be entirely wrong.
- It can also be a complete statement in the form of a question which is answered by choosing one of the statements listed.

- It can be in the form of a problem – again you select the best answer.

Here is an example of a multiple-choice question with a discussion which should give you some clues as to the method for choosing the right answer:

When an employee has a complaint about his assignment, the action which will *best* help him overcome his difficulty is to
- A. discuss his difficulty with his coworkers
- B. take the problem to the head of the organization
- C. take the problem to the person who gave him the assignment
- D. say nothing to anyone about his complaint

In answering this question, you should study each of the choices to find which is best. Consider choice "A" – Certainly an employee may discuss his complaint with fellow employees, but no change or improvement can result, and the complaint remains unresolved. Choice "B" is a poor choice since the head of the organization probably does not know what assignment you have been given, and taking your problem to him is known as "going over the head" of the supervisor. The supervisor, or person who made the assignment, is the person who can clarify it or correct any injustice. Choice "C" is, therefore, correct. To say nothing, as in choice "D," is unwise. Supervisors have and interest in knowing the problems employees are facing, and the employee is seeking a solution to his problem.

2) True/False Questions

The "true/false" or "right/wrong" form of question is sometimes used. Here a complete statement is given. Your job is to decide whether the statement is right or wrong.

SAMPLE: A roaming cell-phone call to a nearby city costs less than a non-roaming call to a distant city.

This statement is wrong, or false, since roaming calls are more expensive.

This is not a complete list of all possible question forms, although most of the others are variations of these common types. You will always get complete directions for answering questions. Be sure you understand *how* to mark your answers – ask questions until you do.

V. RECORDING YOUR ANSWERS

Computer terminals are used more and more today for many different kinds of exams.
For an examination with very few applicants, you may be told to record your answers in the test booklet itself. Separate answer sheets are much more common. If this separate answer sheet is to be scored by machine – and this is often the case – it is highly important that you mark your answers correctly in order to get credit.

An electronic scoring machine is often used in civil service offices because of the speed with which papers can be scored. Machine-scored answer sheets must be marked with a pencil, which will be given to you. This pencil has a high graphite content which responds to the electronic scoring machine. As a matter of fact, stray dots may register as answers, so do not let your pencil rest on the answer sheet while you are pondering the correct answer. Also, if your pencil lead breaks or is otherwise defective, ask for another.

Since the answer sheet will be dropped in a slot in the scoring machine, be careful not to bend the corners or get the paper crumpled.

The answer sheet normally has five vertical columns of numbers, with 30 numbers to a column. These numbers correspond to the question numbers in your test booklet. After each number, going across the page are four or five pairs of dotted lines. These short dotted lines have small letters or numbers above them. The first two pairs may also have a "T" or "F" above the letters. This indicates that the first two pairs only are to be used if the questions are of the true-false type. If the questions are multiple choice, disregard the "T" and "F" and pay attention only to the small letters or numbers.

Answer your questions in the manner of the sample that follows:

32. The largest city in the United States is
 A. Washington, D.C.
 B. New York City
 C. Chicago
 D. Detroit
 E. San Francisco

1) Choose the answer you think is best. (New York City is the largest, so "B" is correct.)
2) Find the row of dotted lines numbered the same as the question you are answering. (Find row number 32)
3) Find the pair of dotted lines corresponding to the answer. (Find the pair of lines under the mark "B.")
4) Make a solid black mark between the dotted lines.

VI. BEFORE THE TEST

Common sense will help you find procedures to follow to get ready for an examination. Too many of us, however, overlook these sensible measures. Indeed, nervousness and fatigue have been found to be the most serious reasons why applicants fail to do their best on civil service tests. Here is a list of reminders:

- Begin your preparation early – Don't wait until the last minute to go scurrying around for books and materials or to find out what the position is all about.
- Prepare continuously – An hour a night for a week is better than an all-night cram session. This has been definitely established. What is more, a night a week for a month will return better dividends than crowding your study into a shorter period of time.
- Locate the place of the exam – You have been sent a notice telling you when and where to report for the examination. If the location is in a different town or otherwise unfamiliar to you, it would be well to inquire the best route and learn something about the building.
- Relax the night before the test – Allow your mind to rest. Do not study at all that night. Plan some mild recreation or diversion; then go to bed early and get a good night's sleep.
- Get up early enough to make a leisurely trip to the place for the test – This way unforeseen events, traffic snarls, unfamiliar buildings, etc. will not upset you.
- Dress comfortably – A written test is not a fashion show. You will be known by number and not by name, so wear something comfortable.

- Leave excess paraphernalia at home – Shopping bags and odd bundles will get in your way. You need bring only the items mentioned in the official notice you received; usually everything you need is provided. Do not bring reference books to the exam. They will only confuse those last minutes and be taken away from you when in the test room.
- Arrive somewhat ahead of time – If because of transportation schedules you must get there very early, bring a newspaper or magazine to take your mind off yourself while waiting.
- Locate the examination room – When you have found the proper room, you will be directed to the seat or part of the room where you will sit. Sometimes you are given a sheet of instructions to read while you are waiting. Do not fill out any forms until you are told to do so; just read them and be prepared.
- Relax and prepare to listen to the instructions
- If you have any physical problem that may keep you from doing your best, be sure to tell the test administrator. If you are sick or in poor health, you really cannot do your best on the exam. You can come back and take the test some other time.

VII. AT THE TEST

The day of the test is here and you have the test booklet in your hand. The temptation to get going is very strong. Caution! There is more to success than knowing the right answers. You must know how to identify your papers and understand variations in the type of short-answer question used in this particular examination. Follow these suggestions for maximum results from your efforts:

1) Cooperate with the monitor

The test administrator has a duty to create a situation in which you can be as much at ease as possible. He will give instructions, tell you when to begin, check to see that you are marking your answer sheet correctly, and so on. He is not there to guard you, although he will see that your competitors do not take unfair advantage. He wants to help you do your best.

2) Listen to all instructions

Don't jump the gun! Wait until you understand all directions. In most civil service tests you get more time than you need to answer the questions. So don't be in a hurry. Read each word of instructions until you clearly understand the meaning. Study the examples, listen to all announcements and follow directions. Ask questions if you do not understand what to do.

3) Identify your papers

Civil service exams are usually identified by number only. You will be assigned a number; you must not put your name on your test papers. Be sure to copy your number correctly. Since more than one exam may be given, copy your exact examination title.

4) Plan your time

Unless you are told that a test is a "speed" or "rate of work" test, speed itself is usually not important. Time enough to answer all the questions will be provided, but this does not mean that you have all day. An overall time limit has been set. Divide the total time (in minutes) by the number of questions to determine the approximate time you have for each question.

5) Do not linger over difficult questions

If you come across a difficult question, mark it with a paper clip (useful to have along) and come back to it when you have been through the booklet. One caution if you do this – be sure to skip a number on your answer sheet as well. Check often to be sure that you have not lost your place and that you are marking in the row numbered the same as the question you are answering.

6) Read the questions

Be sure you know what the question asks! Many capable people are unsuccessful because they failed to *read* the questions correctly.

7) Answer all questions

Unless you have been instructed that a penalty will be deducted for incorrect answers, it is better to guess than to omit a question.

8) Speed tests

It is often better NOT to guess on speed tests. It has been found that on timed tests people are tempted to spend the last few seconds before time is called in marking answers at random – without even reading them – in the hope of picking up a few extra points. To discourage this practice, the instructions may warn you that your score will be "corrected" for guessing. That is, a penalty will be applied. The incorrect answers will be deducted from the correct ones, or some other penalty formula will be used.

9) Review your answers

If you finish before time is called, go back to the questions you guessed or omitted to give them further thought. Review other answers if you have time.

10) Return your test materials

If you are ready to leave before others have finished or time is called, take ALL your materials to the monitor and leave quietly. Never take any test material with you. The monitor can discover whose papers are not complete, and taking a test booklet may be grounds for disqualification.

VIII. EXAMINATION TECHNIQUES

1) Read the general instructions carefully. These are usually printed on the first page of the exam booklet. As a rule, these instructions refer to the timing of the examination; the fact that you should not start work until the signal and must stop work at a signal, etc. If there are any *special* instructions, such as a choice of questions to be answered, make sure that you note this instruction carefully.

2) When you are ready to start work on the examination, that is as soon as the signal has been given, read the instructions to each question booklet, underline any key words or phrases, such as *least, best, outline, describe* and the like. In this way you will tend to answer as requested rather than discover on reviewing your paper that you *listed without describing*, that you selected the *worst* choice rather than the *best* choice, etc.

3) If the examination is of the objective or multiple-choice type – that is, each question will also give a series of possible answers: A, B, C or D, and you are called upon to select the best answer and write the letter next to that answer on your answer paper – it is advisable to start answering each question in turn. There may be anywhere from 50 to 100 such questions in the three or four hours allotted and you can see how much time would be taken if you read through all the questions before beginning to answer any. Furthermore, if you come across a question or group of questions which you know would be difficult to answer, it would undoubtedly affect your handling of all the other questions.

4) If the examination is of the essay type and contains but a few questions, it is a moot point as to whether you should read all the questions before starting to answer any one. Of course, if you are given a choice – say five out of seven and the like – then it is essential to read all the questions so you can eliminate the two that are most difficult. If, however, you are asked to answer all the questions, there may be danger in trying to answer the easiest one first because you may find that you will spend too much time on it. The best technique is to answer the first question, then proceed to the second, etc.

5) Time your answers. Before the exam begins, write down the time it started, then add the time allowed for the examination and write down the time it must be completed, then divide the time available somewhat as follows:
    - If 3-1/2 hours are allowed, that would be 210 minutes. If you have 80 objective-type questions, that would be an average of 2-1/2 minutes per question. Allow yourself no more than 2 minutes per question, or a total of 160 minutes, which will permit about 50 minutes to review.
    - If for the time allotment of 210 minutes there are 7 essay questions to answer, that would average about 30 minutes a question. Give yourself only 25 minutes per question so that you have about 35 minutes to review.

6) The most important instruction is to *read each question* and make sure you know what is wanted. The second most important instruction is to *time yourself properly* so that you answer every question. The third most important instruction is to *answer every question*. Guess if you have to but include something for each question. Remember that you will receive no credit for a blank and will probably receive some credit if you write something in answer to an essay question. If you guess a letter – say "B" for a multiple-choice question – you may have guessed right. If you leave a blank as an answer to a multiple-choice question, the examiners may respect your feelings but it will not add a point to your score. Some exams may penalize you for wrong answers, so in such cases *only*, you may not want to guess unless you have some basis for your answer.

7) Suggestions
    a. Objective-type questions
        1. Examine the question booklet for proper sequence of pages and questions
        2. Read all instructions carefully
        3. Skip any question which seems too difficult; return to it after all other questions have been answered
        4. Apportion your time properly; do not spend too much time on any single question or group of questions

5. Note and underline key words – *all, most, fewest, least, best, worst, same, opposite,* etc.
6. Pay particular attention to negatives
7. Note unusual option, e.g., unduly long, short, complex, different or similar in content to the body of the question
8. Observe the use of "hedging" words – *probably, may, most likely,* etc.
9. Make sure that your answer is put next to the same number as the question
10. Do not second-guess unless you have good reason to believe the second answer is definitely more correct
11. Cross out original answer if you decide another answer is more accurate; do not erase until you are ready to hand your paper in
12. Answer all questions; guess unless instructed otherwise
13. Leave time for review

b. Essay questions
1. Read each question carefully
2. Determine exactly what is wanted. Underline key words or phrases.
3. Decide on outline or paragraph answer
4. Include many different points and elements unless asked to develop any one or two points or elements
5. Show impartiality by giving pros and cons unless directed to select one side only
6. Make and write down any assumptions you find necessary to answer the questions
7. Watch your English, grammar, punctuation and choice of words
8. Time your answers; don't crowd material

8) Answering the essay question

Most essay questions can be answered by framing the specific response around several key words or ideas. Here are a few such key words or ideas:

M's: manpower, materials, methods, money, management
P's: purpose, program, policy, plan, procedure, practice, problems, pitfalls, personnel, public relations

a. Six basic steps in handling problems:
1. Preliminary plan and background development
2. Collect information, data and facts
3. Analyze and interpret information, data and facts
4. Analyze and develop solutions as well as make recommendations
5. Prepare report and sell recommendations
6. Install recommendations and follow up effectiveness

b. Pitfalls to avoid
1. *Taking things for granted* – A statement of the situation does not necessarily imply that each of the elements is necessarily true; for example, a complaint may be invalid and biased so that all that can be taken for granted is that a complaint has been registered

2. *Considering only one side of a situation* – Wherever possible, indicate several alternatives and then point out the reasons you selected the best one
3. *Failing to indicate follow up* – Whenever your answer indicates action on your part, make certain that you will take proper follow-up action to see how successful your recommendations, procedures or actions turn out to be
4. *Taking too long in answering any single question* – Remember to time your answers properly

IX. AFTER THE TEST

Scoring procedures differ in detail among civil service jurisdictions although the general principles are the same. Whether the papers are hand-scored or graded by machine we have described, they are nearly always graded by number. That is, the person who marks the paper knows only the number – never the name – of the applicant. Not until all the papers have been graded will they be matched with names. If other tests, such as training and experience or oral interview ratings have been given, scores will be combined. Different parts of the examination usually have different weights. For example, the written test might count 60 percent of the final grade, and a rating of training and experience 40 percent. In many jurisdictions, veterans will have a certain number of points added to their grades.

After the final grade has been determined, the names are placed in grade order and an eligible list is established. There are various methods for resolving ties between those who get the same final grade – probably the most common is to place first the name of the person whose application was received first. Job offers are made from the eligible list in the order the names appear on it. You will be notified of your grade and your rank as soon as all these computations have been made. This will be done as rapidly as possible.

People who are found to meet the requirements in the announcement are called "eligibles." Their names are put on a list of eligible candidates. An eligible's chances of getting a job depend on how high he stands on this list and how fast agencies are filling jobs from the list.

When a job is to be filled from a list of eligibles, the agency asks for the names of people on the list of eligibles for that job. When the civil service commission receives this request, it sends to the agency the names of the three people highest on this list. Or, if the job to be filled has specialized requirements, the office sends the agency the names of the top three persons who meet these requirements from the general list.

The appointing officer makes a choice from among the three people whose names were sent to him. If the selected person accepts the appointment, the names of the others are put back on the list to be considered for future openings.

That is the rule in hiring from all kinds of eligible lists, whether they are for typist, carpenter, chemist, or something else. For every vacancy, the appointing officer has his choice of any one of the top three eligibles on the list. This explains why the person whose name is on top of the list sometimes does not get an appointment when some of the persons lower on the list do. If the appointing officer chooses the second or third eligible, the No. 1 eligible does not get a job at once, but stays on the list until he is appointed or the list is terminated.

X. HOW TO PASS THE INTERVIEW TEST

The examination for which you applied requires an oral interview test. You have already taken the written test and you are now being called for the interview test – the final part of the formal examination.

You may think that it is not possible to prepare for an interview test and that there are no procedures to follow during an interview. Our purpose is to point out some things you can do in advance that will help you and some good rules to follow and pitfalls to avoid while you are being interviewed.

What is an interview supposed to test?

The written examination is designed to test the technical knowledge and competence of the candidate; the oral is designed to evaluate intangible qualities, not readily measured otherwise, and to establish a list showing the relative fitness of each candidate – as measured against his competitors – for the position sought. Scoring is not on the basis of "right" and "wrong," but on a sliding scale of values ranging from "not passable" to "outstanding." As a matter of fact, it is possible to achieve a relatively low score without a single "incorrect" answer because of evident weakness in the qualities being measured.

Occasionally, an examination may consist entirely of an oral test – either an individual or a group oral. In such cases, information is sought concerning the technical knowledges and abilities of the candidate, since there has been no written examination for this purpose. More commonly, however, an oral test is used to supplement a written examination.

Who conducts interviews?

The composition of oral boards varies among different jurisdictions. In nearly all, a representative of the personnel department serves as chairman. One of the members of the board may be a representative of the department in which the candidate would work. In some cases, "outside experts" are used, and, frequently, a businessman or some other representative of the general public is asked to serve. Labor and management or other special groups may be represented. The aim is to secure the services of experts in the appropriate field.

However the board is composed, it is a good idea (and not at all improper or unethical) to ascertain in advance of the interview who the members are and what groups they represent. When you are introduced to them, you will have some idea of their backgrounds and interests, and at least you will not stutter and stammer over their names.

What should be done before the interview?

While knowledge about the board members is useful and takes some of the surprise element out of the interview, there is other preparation which is more substantive. It *is* possible to prepare for an oral interview – in several ways:

1) **Keep a copy of your application and review it carefully before the interview**

This may be the only document before the oral board, and the starting point of the interview. Know what education and experience you have listed there, and the sequence and dates of all of it. Sometimes the board will ask you to review the highlights of your experience for them; you should not have to hem and haw doing it.

2) **Study the class specification and the examination announcement**

Usually, the oral board has one or both of these to guide them. The qualities, characteristics or knowledges required by the position sought are stated in these documents. They offer valuable clues as to the nature of the oral interview. For example, if the job involves supervisory responsibilities, the announcement will usually indicate that knowledge of modern supervisory methods and the qualifications of the candidate as a supervisor will be tested. If so, you can expect such questions, frequently in the form of a hypothetical situation which you are expected to solve. NEVER go into an oral without knowledge of the duties and responsibilities of the job you seek.

3) Think through each qualification required

Try to visualize the kind of questions you would ask if you were a board member. How well could you answer them? Try especially to appraise your own knowledge and background in each area, *measured against the job sought*, and identify any areas in which you are weak. Be critical and realistic – do not flatter yourself.

4) Do some general reading in areas in which you feel you may be weak

For example, if the job involves supervision and your past experience has NOT, some general reading in supervisory methods and practices, particularly in the field of human relations, might be useful. Do NOT study agency procedures or detailed manuals. The oral board will be testing your understanding and capacity, not your memory.

5) Get a good night's sleep and watch your general health and mental attitude

You will want a clear head at the interview. Take care of a cold or any other minor ailment, and of course, no hangovers.

What should be done on the day of the interview?

Now comes the day of the interview itself. Give yourself plenty of time to get there. Plan to arrive somewhat ahead of the scheduled time, particularly if your appointment is in the fore part of the day. If a previous candidate fails to appear, the board might be ready for you a bit early. By early afternoon an oral board is almost invariably behind schedule if there are many candidates, and you may have to wait. Take along a book or magazine to read, or your application to review, but leave any extraneous material in the waiting room when you go in for your interview. In any event, relax and compose yourself.

The matter of dress is important. The board is forming impressions about you – from your experience, your manners, your attitude, and your appearance. Give your personal appearance careful attention. Dress your best, but not your flashiest. Choose conservative, appropriate clothing, and be sure it is immaculate. This is a business interview, and your appearance should indicate that you regard it as such. Besides, being well groomed and properly dressed will help boost your confidence.

Sooner or later, someone will call your name and escort you into the interview room. *This is it.* From here on you are on your own. It is too late for any more preparation. But remember, you asked for this opportunity to prove your fitness, and you are here because your request was granted.

What happens when you go in?

The usual sequence of events will be as follows: The clerk (who is often the board stenographer) will introduce you to the chairman of the oral board, who will introduce you to the other members of the board. Acknowledge the introductions before you sit down. Do not be surprised if you find a microphone facing you or a stenotypist sitting by. Oral interviews are usually recorded in the event of an appeal or other review.

Usually the chairman of the board will open the interview by reviewing the highlights of your education and work experience from your application – primarily for the benefit of the other members of the board, as well as to get the material into the record. Do not interrupt or comment unless there is an error or significant misinterpretation; if that is the case, do not hesitate. But do not quibble about insignificant matters. Also, he will usually ask you some question about your education, experience or your present job – partly to get you to start talking and to establish the interviewing "rapport." He may start the actual questioning, or turn it over to one of the other members. Frequently, each member undertakes the questioning on a particular area, one in which he is perhaps most competent, so you can expect each member to participate in the examination. Because time is limited, you may also expect some rather abrupt switches in the direction the questioning takes, so do not be upset by it. Normally, a board member will not pursue a single line of questioning unless he discovers a particular strength or weakness.

After each member has participated, the chairman will usually ask whether any member has any further questions, then will ask you if you have anything you wish to add. Unless you are expecting this question, it may floor you. Worse, it may start you off on an extended, extemporaneous speech. The board is not usually seeking more information. The question is principally to offer you a last opportunity to present further qualifications or to indicate that you have nothing to add. So, if you feel that a significant qualification or characteristic has been overlooked, it is proper to point it out in a sentence or so. Do not compliment the board on the thoroughness of their examination – they have been sketchy, and you know it. If you wish, merely say, "No thank you, I have nothing further to add." This is a point where you can "talk yourself out" of a good impression or fail to present an important bit of information. Remember, *you close the interview yourself.*

The chairman will then say, "That is all, Mr. _____, thank you." Do not be startled; the interview is over, and quicker than you think. Thank him, gather your belongings and take your leave. Save your sigh of relief for the other side of the door.

How to put your best foot forward
Throughout this entire process, you may feel that the board individually and collectively is trying to pierce your defenses, seek out your hidden weaknesses and embarrass and confuse you. Actually, this is not true. They are obliged to make an appraisal of your qualifications for the job you are seeking, and they want to see you in your best light. Remember, they must interview all candidates and a non-cooperative candidate may become a failure in spite of their best efforts to bring out his qualifications. Here are 15 suggestions that will help you:

1) **Be natural – Keep your attitude confident, not cocky**
If you are not confident that you can do the job, do not expect the board to be. Do not apologize for your weaknesses, try to bring out your strong points. The board is interested in a positive, not negative, presentation. Cockiness will antagonize any board member and make him wonder if you are covering up a weakness by a false show of strength.

2) **Get comfortable, but don't lounge or sprawl**
Sit erectly but not stiffly. A careless posture may lead the board to conclude that you are careless in other things, or at least that you are not impressed by the importance of the occasion. Either conclusion is natural, even if incorrect. Do not fuss with your clothing, a pencil or an ashtray. Your hands may occasionally be useful to emphasize a point; do not let them become a point of distraction.

3) **Do not wisecrack or make small talk**
This is a serious situation, and your attitude should show that you consider it as such. Further, the time of the board is limited – they do not want to waste it, and neither should you.

4) Do not exaggerate your experience or abilities

In the first place, from information in the application or other interviews and sources, the board may know more about you than you think. Secondly, you probably will not get away with it. An experienced board is rather adept at spotting such a situation, so do not take the chance.

5) If you know a board member, do not make a point of it, yet do not hide it

Certainly you are not fooling him, and probably not the other members of the board. Do not try to take advantage of your acquaintanceship – it will probably do you little good.

6) Do not dominate the interview

Let the board do that. They will give you the clues – do not assume that you have to do all the talking. Realize that the board has a number of questions to ask you, and do not try to take up all the interview time by showing off your extensive knowledge of the answer to the first one.

7) Be attentive

You only have 20 minutes or so, and you should keep your attention at its sharpest throughout. When a member is addressing a problem or question to you, give him your undivided attention. Address your reply principally to him, but do not exclude the other board members.

8) Do not interrupt

A board member may be stating a problem for you to analyze. He will ask you a question when the time comes. Let him state the problem, and wait for the question.

9) Make sure you understand the question

Do not try to answer until you are sure what the question is. If it is not clear, restate it in your own words or ask the board member to clarify it for you. However, do not haggle about minor elements.

10) Reply promptly but not hastily

A common entry on oral board rating sheets is "candidate responded readily," or "candidate hesitated in replies." Respond as promptly and quickly as you can, but do not jump to a hasty, ill-considered answer.

11) Do not be peremptory in your answers

A brief answer is proper – but do not fire your answer back. That is a losing game from your point of view. The board member can probably ask questions much faster than you can answer them.

12) Do not try to create the answer you think the board member wants

He is interested in what kind of mind you have and how it works – not in playing games. Furthermore, he can usually spot this practice and will actually grade you down on it.

13) Do not switch sides in your reply merely to agree with a board member

Frequently, a member will take a contrary position merely to draw you out and to see if you are willing and able to defend your point of view. Do not start a debate, yet do not surrender a good position. If a position is worth taking, it is worth defending.

14) Do not be afraid to admit an error in judgment if you are shown to be wrong

The board knows that you are forced to reply without any opportunity for careful consideration. Your answer may be demonstrably wrong. If so, admit it and get on with the interview.

15) Do not dwell at length on your present job

The opening question may relate to your present assignment. Answer the question but do not go into an extended discussion. You are being examined for a *new* job, not your present one. As a matter of fact, try to phrase ALL your answers in terms of the job for which you are being examined.

Basis of Rating

Probably you will forget most of these "do's" and "don'ts" when you walk into the oral interview room. Even remembering them all will not ensure you a passing grade. Perhaps you did not have the qualifications in the first place. But remembering them will help you to put your best foot forward, without treading on the toes of the board members.

Rumor and popular opinion to the contrary notwithstanding, an oral board wants you to make the best appearance possible. They know you are under pressure – but they also want to see how you respond to it as a guide to what your reaction would be under the pressures of the job you seek. They will be influenced by the degree of poise you display, the personal traits you show and the manner in which you respond.

ABOUT THIS BOOK

This book contains tests divided into Examination Sections. Go through each test, answering every question in the margin. We have also attached a sample answer sheet at the back of the book that can be removed and used. At the end of each test look at the answer key and check your answers. On the ones you got wrong, look at the right answer choice and learn. Do not fill in the answers first. Do not memorize the questions and answers, but understand the answer and principles involved. On your test, the questions will likely be different from the samples. Questions are changed and new ones added. If you understand these past questions you should have success with any changes that arise. Tests may consist of several types of questions. We have additional books on each subject should more study be advisable or necessary for you. Finally, the more you study, the better prepared you will be. This book is intended to be the last thing you study before you walk into the examination room. Prior study of relevant texts is also recommended. NLC publishes some of these in our Fundamental Series. Knowledge and good sense are important factors in passing your exam. Good luck also helps. So now study this Passbook, absorb the material contained within and take that knowledge into the examination. Then do your best to pass that exam.

EXAMINATION SECTION

EXAMINATION SECTION

TEST 1

DIRECTIONS: Each question or incomplete statement is followed by several suggested answers or completions. Select the one that BEST answers the question or completes the statement. *PRINT THE LETTER OF THE CORRECT ANSWER IN THE SPACE AT THE RIGHT.*

1. If a Private Patrol Operator wishes to work armed, how much insurance coverage is he/she required to carry?
   A. $250,000 B. $500,000 C. $1,000,000 D. $2,000,000

   1.____

2. If the vehicle of a Private Patrol Operator is equipped with an amber lightbar, how much must this vehicle be marked?
   A. Company name on doors and rear
   B. Company name on side doors, security on the rear
   C. Company logo on sides, PPO license number on rear
   D. Private Security or Security Patrol on both sides and on rear

   2.____

3. How many hours of training must a Private Patrol Operator undergo if he/she wants to carry tear gas or other chemical spray?
   A. 2 B. 4 C. 6 D. 8

   3.____

4. A Private Patrol Operator is required to keep the I-9 form of an ex-employee for what period of time?
   A. One year after the end of employment
   B. Three years after the end of employment
   C. Whichever is longer: three years from hire date or year from exit date
   D. Whichever is longer: five years from hire date or three years from exit date

   4.____

5. If a Private Patrol Operator changes residence address or business address, they must notify the Bureau of Security and Investigative Services within a time period of _____ days.
   A. 10 B. 30 C. 60 D. 90

   5.____

6. A firearms qualification card expires at a time period of _____ year(s) from the date of issuance if not renewed.
   A. 1 B. 2 C. 3 D. 5

   6.____

7. The fine for a misdemeanor violation of offering Private Patrol Operator services without a Private Patrol Operator license is what dollar amount?
   A. $1,000 B. $5,000 C. $10,000 D. $20,000

   7.____

8. Carrying a gun concealed under a shirt is usually what type of crime?
   A. Felony
   B. Misdemeanor
   C. Summary offense
   D. Inchoate crime

   8.____

9. Carrying a set of "brass knuckles" in your pocket is usually what type of crime?
   A. Felony
   B. Misdemeanor
   C. Summary offense
   D. Inchoate crime

10. If a person is convicted of providing Private Patrol Operator services without a license, he/she cannot be issued a Private Patrol Operator license for what time period following a conviction?
    A. 90 days
    B. 120 days
    C. 6 months
    D. 12 months

11. If a person is convicted a second time for providing Private Patrol Operator services without a license, he/she cannot be issued a PPO license for what period of time following the second conviction?
    A. 3 years
    B. 5 years
    C. 10 years
    D. 15 years

12. What is the fine if a Private Patrol Operator license is not properly posted?
    A. $250
    B. $500
    C. $1,000
    D. $2,500

13. The shoulder patch required to be on a Private Patrol Operator's security uniform must bear what two pieces of information?
    A. The words "Private Security" and the guard's name
    B. The guard's name and identification number
    C. The words "Private Security" and the guard's identification number
    D. The words "Private Security" and the name of the private patrol company the guard represents

14. In order to become a Private Patrol Operator, applicants should meet what minimum experience requirement?
    _____ of experience as a patrol person, guard, or watchman
    A. 6 months
    B. 1 year
    C. 2 years
    D. 3 years

15. If a Private Patrol Operator or an employee of a Private Patrol Operator discharges a firearm with the scope and course of his/her duty, a report of the incident must be provided to the Director of BSIS within what time frame?
    A. 24 hours
    B. 3 days
    C. 5 days
    D. 7 days

16. A Private Patrol Operator's application for a Private Patrol Operator license is considered to be "abandoned" if not completed within what time period of it being initially filed?
    A. 30 days
    B. 6 days
    C. 90 days
    D. 1 year

17. What is the MINIMUM number of hours of instruction required for a baton class?
    A. 4
    B. 6
    C. 8
    D. 12

18. If a guard quits working for a Private Patrol Operator without giving notice, when must the guard be given his/her final pay?
    A. Immediately
    B. Within 72 hours
    C. Within 7 days
    D. On the next scheduled payday

19. If a guard working for a Private Patrol Operator is fired by the Private Patrol Operator, when must the guard be given his/her final pay?
    A. Immediately
    B. Within 72 hours
    C. Within 7 days
    D. On the next scheduled payday

20. Private Patrol Operator vehicles bearing amber colored lights must have markings in a size in which they are legible from a distance of _____ feet.
    A. 10 B. 25 C. 50 D. 100

21. What is the MAXIMUM time frame in which a Private Patrol Operator license can be expired and still be eligible for renewal?
    A. 30 days B. 1 year C. 2 years D. 3 years

22. How many employees (or more) must a Private Patrol Operator company have in order for supervisors to be required by law to attend sexual harassment training?
    A. 5 B. 10 C. 25 D. 50

23. How often and for what time period is sexual harassment training required for supervisors who are required to attend?
    A. 2 hours every year
    B. 2 hours every 2 years
    C. 4 hours every 2 years
    D. 8 hours every 2 years

24. Which of the following roles is required when advertising for another location, or conducting business from, other than the Private Patrol Operator's primary business location?
    A. Branch officer
    B. Exclusive officer
    C. Proprietary officer
    D. Managing officer

25. How many employees can a Private Patrol Operator employ before being required to have a workers' compensation insurance policy?
    A. 0 B. 5 C. 10 D. 50

KEY (CORRECT ANSWERS)

1. C
2. D
3. A
4. C
5. B

6. B
7. C
8. B
9. A
10. D

11. B
12. A
13. D
14. B
15. D

16. D
17. C
18. B
19. A
20. C

21. D
22. D
23. B
24. A
25. A

TEST 2

DIRECTIONS: Each question or incomplete statement is followed by several suggested answers or completions. Select the one that BEST answers the question or completes the statement. *PRINT THE LETTER OF THE CORRECT ANSWER IN THE SPACE AT THE RIGHT.*

1. If a Private Patrol Operator dies, for what time period may the Private Patrol Operator's immediate family operate the business of the deceased Private Patrol Operator?
   A. 7 days   B. 30 days   C. 90 days   D. 120 days

   1._____

2. What is the proper name for an arrest made by a guard?
   A. Citizen's arrest
   B. Certified arrest
   C. Personal arrest
   D. Private person arrest

   2._____

3. What IRS form would you use to report payments made to a regular employee?
   A. I-9   B. W-2   C. W-4   D. W-9

   3._____

4. What type of form would be used by the employer to verify an employee's identity and to establish that the worker is eligible to accept employment in the United States?
   A. I-9   B. W-2   C. W-4   D. W-9

   4._____

5. If a guard discharges his/her firearm while on duty, within what time period must the guard report this to his/her employer?
   A. 24 hours   B. 3 days   C. 5 days   D. 7 days

   5._____

6. During the initial 40 hours of training for a new guard, _____ hours should be devoted to terrorism awareness and weapons of mass destruction.
   A. 2   B. 4   C. 6   D. 8

   6._____

7. A Type _____ extinguisher would be used on an electrical fire.
   A. A   B. B   C. C   D. D

   7._____

8. What self-defense weapon can a guard carry with no permit required?
   A. Tear gas
   B. Baton
   C. Electrical stun gun
   D. Unconcealed pistol

   8._____

9. What penalty may a Private Patrol Operator incur if he/she has been found to have committed "dishonesty" or "fraud"?
   A. $250 fine
   B. Up to a year of incarceration
   C. More than a year of incarceration
   D. Suspension or revocation of the PPO license

   9._____

10. If a person is hyperventilating, is unresponsive to touch, has cold skin, and is extremely talkative, what medical condition is this person likely experiencing?
    A. Shock
    B. Cardiac arrest
    C. Asthma attack
    D. Hypoglycemia

    10._____

11. What IRS form is used by many Private Patrol Operators in a fraudulent attempt to get around laws involving payroll taxes and workers compensation insurance?
    A. I-9
    B. W-4
    C. W-9
    D. 1099

    11._____

12. If a representative of a Private Patrol Operator company is involved in any way in the unlawful listening or recording of telephone calls, which of the following has he/she violated?
    A. Personal privacy
    B. PPO Code of Ethics
    C. Law enforcement regulations
    D. State and federal laws

    12._____

13. What two cards must a security officer have in his/her possession while carrying a firearm on duty?
    A. Driver's license and guard card
    B. Driver's license and FQ card
    C. Guard card and FQ card
    D. Guard card and Social Security card

    13._____

14. What equipment is NOT permitted to be a part of a security company's vehicles?
    A. Cellular phones
    B. Distinctive markings
    C. Amber lights
    D. Sirens

    14._____

15. What are the counter-terrorism techniques known as "The 4 D's" that can be performed by a security guard?
    Deter,
    A. delay, deny, and detect
    B. distinguish, detract, and delay
    C. distinguish, deny, and delay
    D. detract, defense, and deny

    15._____

16. Companies with how many employees are permitted to have oral and not written emergency action plans?
    A. 0-10
    B. 10-25
    C. 26-50
    D. 51 or more

    16._____

17. Why is it required to report new employees or re-hired employees to the State?
    A. So employee time counts toward Social Security benefits
    B. So employee can be required to pay taxes
    C. So the employee can no longer be counted in unemployment statistics
    D. So the employee can be made responsible for unpaid child support

    17._____

18. If a Private Patrol Operator or a security officer wants to obtain an exposed-weapon FQ firearms-carry card, how many hours of training are required?
    A. 8
    B. 14
    C. 20
    D. 40

    18._____

19. What are the three main parts of basic protective measures?
    A. Rescue, alarm, and contain
    B. Promote, prevent, protect
    C. Time, distance, and shielding
    D. Knowledge, planning, execution

20. What is the first line of defense for all emergency situations?
    A. Reaction   B. Preparation   C. Evacuation   D. Leadership

21. All of the following items of information are included on a Firearm Carry card issued from the Bureau of Security and Investigative Services EXCEPT
    A. applicant's name
    B. Caliber of weapon
    C. Expiration date
    D. Applicant's Social Security number

22. What government agency has the ability to fine a Private Patrol Operator for I-0 non-compliance?
    A. Department of Labor
    B. Department of Homeland Security
    C. Occupational Safety and Health Administration
    D. Environmental Protection Agency

23. A security officer has all of the following in his/her possession in order to be hired on the spot by a Private Patrol Operator EXCEPT
    A. current identification
    B. current guard card
    C. current driver's license
    D. legal lability to work in the United States

24. What is the name of the legal document a Private Patrol Operator should obtain from a client and give photocopies of it to on-site guards, that allows towing companies to tow away illegally parked vehicles on the client's private property?
    A. Advance directive
    B. Power of attorney
    C. Right to privacy
    D. Proof of ownership

25. A law enforcement agent inducing a person to commit an offense that the person would otherwise have been unlikely to commit may be found guilty of which of the following?
    A. Coercion
    B. Entrapment
    C. Collusion
    D. Insubordination

KEY (CORRECT ANSWERS)

1. D
2. D
3. B
4. A
5. A

6. B
7. C
8. C
9. D
10. A

11. D
12. D
13. C
14. D
15. A

16. A
17. D
18. B
19. C
20. B

21. D
22. B
23. C
24. B
25. B

TEST 3

DIRECTIONS: Each question or incomplete statement is followed by several suggested answers or completions. Select the one that BEST answers the question or completes the statement. *PRINT THE LETTER OF THE CORRECT ANSWER IN THE SPACE AT THE RIGHT.*

1. The application and examination fee for an original Private Patrol Operator license may NOT exceed what dollar amount?
   A. $100   B. $250   C. $500   D. $1,000

2. A registration fee for a guard may NOT exceed what dollar amount?
   A. $10   B. $25   C. $50   D. $100

3. Who has the ultimate authority over what badge a Private Patrol Operator and his/her guards use when working?
   A. Local law enforcement
   B. Department of Homeland Security
   C. Occupational Safety and Health Administration
   D. Bureau of Security and Investigative Services

4. What agency regulates guard choices such as uniform color, badge types, and shoulder patches?
   A. Department of Labor
   B. Department of Homeland Security
   C. Occupational Safety and Health Administration
   D. Bureau of Security and Investigative Services

5. What state agency regulates employee-pay issues?
   A. Department of Labor
   B. Department of Industrial Relations
   C. Occupational Safety and Health Administration
   D. Bureau of Security and Investigative Services

6. Type _____ is a type of fire extinguisher used on a paper or wood fire.
   A. A   B. B   C. C   D. D

7. How many hours of CPR/first aid training does BSIS advise for a security officer?
   A. 2   B. 4   C. 6   D. 8

8. Type _____ is a type of fire extinguisher used on a liquid fire.
   A. A   B. B   C. C   D. D

9. Which of the following is permitted to carry a baton without a BSIS permit?
   A. Branch officer   B. Qualified manager
   C. Proprietary officer   D. Peace officer

10. A _____ arrest refers to a person being held in custody without probable cause or without an order issued by a court of competent jurisdiction.
    A. citizen's   B. certified   C. false   D. private person

11. If a firearm connected to a Private Patrol Operator or any of his/her staff becomes missing, or stolen while on duty, within what time frame must this be reported to local law enforcement?
    A. 24 hours   B. 3 days   C. 5 days   D. 7 days

12. What does the term "brandishing a weapon" mean?
    A. Carrying a concealed weapon
    B. Carrying an unconcealed weapon
    C. Carrying an unregistered weapon
    D. Drawing a weapon in a threatening manner

13. If a security officer is assigned to work a private party and someone uninvited attends and refuses to leave, what can the security officer do in this situation?
    A. Physically remove the person
    B. Arrest for trespass
    C. Arrest for disturbing the peace
    D. Hold the person at gunpoint until the peace officers arrive

14. All of the following should be included on a written report EXCEPT
    A. why it occurred
    B. where it occurred
    C. when it occurred
    D. witnesses to the occurrence

15. What agency requires companies such as construction sites, chemical companies, and refineries to have emergency action plans?
    A. Department of Labor
    B. Department of Industrial Relations
    C. Occupational Safety and Health Administration
    D. Bureau of Security and Investigative Services

16. When writing a proposal to a potential client, what is the MAIN item a Private Patrol Operator should be considering?
    A. Profit margin
    B. Needs of the client
    C. Fatigue of the protecting officers
    D. Environment needing to be protected

17. If a Private Patrol Operator allows one of his/her security officers to carry a baton without a permit, what fine should the PPO expect from BSIS?
    A. $1,000   B. $2,500   C. $5,000   D. $10,000

18. Penal Code _____ is a rule or law that allows a security officer to make an arrest.
    A. 187   B. 242   C. 459   D. 837

19. What IRS payroll form does an employee complete that tells how many exemptions that employee claims to have?
    A. I-9 B. W-4 C. W-9 D. 1099

20. If a Private Patrol Operator's Quality Manager resigns from the company, the non-QM PPO company owner must notify BSIS within _____ days.
    A. 7 B. 30 C. 60 D. 90

21. A guard should renew his/her guard card _____ days prior to the expiration date.
    A. 10-20 B. 30-45 C. 45-60 D. 60-90

22. A security officer can only frisk a person for being in possession of which of the following?
    A. Drugs B. Money C. Weapons D. Stolen items

23. What is the rule on bullet capacity for semi-automatic pistols carried by guards and Private Patrol Operators?
    No more than _____ bullets.
    A. 6 B. 8 C. 10 D. 12

24. If a business wants to employ their own security officer instead of hiring a Private Patrol Operator to supply a guard, that business must register as a Proprietary Private Security Employer. What is the cost of this registration?
    A. $50 B. $75 C. $100 D. $250

25. Which of the following should never be kept in an employee's personnel file?
    A. W-4 form
    B. I-9 form
    C. Employee resume
    D. Performance evaluations

KEY (CORRECT ANSWERS)

1.	C	11.	D
2.	C	12.	D
3.	A	13.	B
4.	D	14.	A
5.	B	15.	C
6.	A	16.	A
7.	A	17.	B
8.	B	18.	D
9.	D	19.	B
10.	C	20.	B

21. D
22. C
23. C
24. B
25. B

TEST 4

DIRECTIONS: Each question or incomplete statement is followed by several suggested answers or completions. Select the one that BEST answers the question or completes the statement. *PRINT THE LETTER OF THE CORRECT ANSWER IN THE SPACE AT THE RIGHT.*

1. What document will a bank require you to present if you want a checking account in the name of your Private Patrol Operator company?
   A. Guard card
   B. I-9 form
   C. Company tax ID number
   D. Fictitious business name filing

   1.____

2. If a Private Patrol Operator contracts with a K-12 school district, the guard has special training requirements if they are on the school campus more than how many hours per week?
   A. 10
   B. 20
   C. 30
   D. 40

   2.____

3. What type of weapons of mass destruction is known to have trigger methods that can be chemical, electronic, or mechanical?
   A. Nuclear
   B. Chemical
   C. Biological
   D. Incendiary

   3.____

4. What two conditions must be present before a suspect can be arrested for a felony?
   The felony must have been
   A. attempted and it must have been witnessed by another individual
   B. witnessed by the individual making the arrest and there must be evidence to support the arrest
   C. committed and there must be reasonable cause that the suspect actually committed the crime
   D. committed or attempted and there must be reasonable cause that the suspect actually committed the crime

   4.____

5. Which of the following BEST describes the authority of a security guard to question an individual on his/her employer's private property?
   The security
   A. guard has the same rights as a private citizen when it comes to questioning others
   B. guard's right to question an individual is equivalent to the rights of a peace officer
   C. guard is not authorized to question an individual on his/her employer's property
   D. guard has the same right as his or her employer and more rights than that of a private citizen

   5.____

6. Which of the following statements are TRUE regarding searching a suspect?
   A. Searching a suspect should be avoided
   B. Searches are performed to find evidence
   C. Suspects do not have rights in regards to being searched
   D. A search should be conducted before the suspect is placed under arrest

   6.____

13

7. When is a security guard required to make an arrest?
   A. Anytime he/she witnesses a violation occurring
   B. When he/she witnesses an individual stealing merchandise
   C. When he/she witnesses a felony occur
   D. A security guard is never required to make an arrest

8. In order for a security guard to prevent offenses from occurring, he/she should be
   A. undercover
   B. highly visible
   C. creating diversions
   D. watching surveillance monitors

9. If you are the only security guard on duty and your assignment is to patrol a warehouse every night, you witness three men coming into the back of the warehouse with firearms.
   What should you do in this situation?
   A. Apprehend the three men and call the police
   B. Call the police but continue observing the men
   C. Go out the front door to save yourself from being seen
   D. Question the men and ask why they are entering the building

10. Smoking on public transportation and speeding are examples of which type of arrestable offense?
    A. Felony   B. Infraction   C. Malfeasance   D. Misdemeanor

11. A registered employee, a Private Patrol Operator, or an alarm company may carry all of the following EXCEPT
    A. baton
    B. knife
    C. firearm
    D. simulated firearm

12. Mustard, cyanide, and chlorine are examples of what type of weapon of mass destruction?
    A. Nuclear   B. Explosive   C. Chemical   D. Incendiary

13. What type of weapon of mass destruction creates fire and is easily made from home-made materials?
    A. Nuclear   B. Explosive   C. Chemical   D. Incendiary

14. The reactionary distance that a security guard should keep between his/her adversary is _____ feet.
    A. 2-4   B. 4-6   C. 6-8   D. 8-10

15. Which of the following offenses is punishable by a modest monetary fine?
    A. Felony   B. Assault   C. Infraction   D. Misdemeanor

16. Which of the following statements are TRUE regarding the offense of trespass?
    A. It is a contract law offense and is always prosecuted.
    B. It is a civil offense and security officers cannot make an arrest.
    C. It is a criminal offense and only police officers can make an arrest.
    D. Security officers should immediately arrest trespassers and then hand them over to the police.

17. What should a security guard do if a site visitor refuses to be searched?
    A. Make an arrest and call the police
    B. Let them go but refuse admittance to the property
    C. Note the person's refusal but allow them onto the property
    D. Hold the person's property and call a manager for assistance

18. Assault is considered to be an offense of _____ law.
    A. tort   B. civil   C. contract   D. criminal

19. Which of the following must a security officer have in his/her possession at all times while on patrol?
    A. Site map   B. Notebook
    C. Handcuffs   D. Incident record book

20. In what circumstance might the use of force be deemed unreasonable? When it is used to
    A. make an arrest
    B. carry out a search
    C. prevent or stop a crime
    D. protect yourself or another individual

21. What is the FIRST thing an officer should do if unauthorized property is discovered during a search?
    A. Deny site access and hold on to the property in question
    B. File a police report but allow the person to retain the property
    C. Give the unauthorized property back but request off-site disposal
    D. Request to know why the person is in possession of the property

22. What is the security officer's FIRST priority when on patrol?
    A. Preserving site integrity
    B. Ensuring their own safety
    C. Ensuring the health and safety of others
    D. Preventing property loss and damage

23. Which of the following statements is TRUE regarding confidential information?
    A. It can be discussed with trusted friends, family, and co-workers.
    B. The consequences of disclosing such information can be serious.
    C. Disclosing such information to unauthorized persons is acceptable.
    D. Holding confidential information is unnecessary for a security officer.

24. Which of the following statements is TRUE regarding incident reports?
    A. The report must contain the home addresses of all parties involved.
    B. Signing and dating is the responsibility of the officer completing the report.
    C. At least one other security officer must witness incident report completion.
    D. It is acceptable for an officer not involved in the incident to complete the report.

25. When an arrest is required, which of the following must be provided to the individual under arrest?
    A. The location of their detainment
    B. Details regarding their statutory rights
    C. The reason for which they are being arrested
    D. Telephone access for calling legal representation

KEY (CORRECT ANSWERS)

1.	D		11.	D
2.	B		12.	C
3.	D		13.	D
4.	C		14.	C
5.	D		15.	C
6.	A		16.	C
7.	D		17.	B
8.	B		18.	D
9.	B		19.	B
10.	B		20.	B

21.	D
22.	B
23.	B
24.	B
25.	B

EXAMINATION SECTION
TEST 1

DIRECTIONS: Questions 1 through 5 are to be answered on the basis of the information, instructions, and sample question given below. Each question contains a GENERAL RULE, EXCEPTIONS, a PROBLEM, and the ACTION actually taken.

The GENERAL RULE explains what the special officer (security officer) should or should not do.

The EXCEPTIONS describe circumstances under which a special officer (security officer) should take action contrary to the GENERAL RULE.

However, an unusual emergency may justify taking an action that is not covered either by the GENERAL RULE or by the stated EXCEPTIONS.

The PROBLEM describes a situation requiring some action by the special officer (security officer).

ACTION describes what a special officer (security officer) actually did in that particular case.

Read carefully the GENERAL RULE and EXCEPTIONS, the PROBLEM, and the ACTION, and the mark A, B, C, or D in the space at the right in accordance with the following instructions:

  I. If an action is clearly justified under the general rule, mark your answer A.
  II. If an action is not justified under the general rule, but is justified under a stated exception, mark your answer B.
  III. If an action is not justified either by the general rule or by a stated exception, but does seem strongly justified by an unusual emergency situation, mark your answer C.
  IV. If an action does not seem justified for any of these reasons, mark your answer D.

SAMPLE QUESTION:

GENERAL RULE: A special officer (security officer) is not empowered to stop a person and search him for hidden weapons.
EXCEPTION: He may stop a person and search him if he has good reason to believe that he may be carrying a hidden weapon. Good reasons to believe he may be carrying a hidden weapon include (a) notification through official channels that a person may be armed, (b) a statement directly to the special officer (security officer) by the person himself that he is armed, and (c) the special officer's (security officer's) own direct observation.

PROBLEM: A special officer (security officer) on duty at a hospital clinic is notified by a woman patient at the clinic that a man sitting near her is making muttered threats that he has a gun and is going to shoot his doctor if the doctor gives him any trouble. Although the woman is upset, she seems to be telling the truth, and two other waiting patients con-

firm this. However, the special officer (security officer) approaches the man and sees no sign of a hidden weapon. The man tells the officer that he has no weapon.
ACTION: The special officer (security officer) takes the man aside into an empty office and proceeds to frisk him for a concealed weapon.

ANSWER: The answer cannot be A, because the general rule is that a special officer (security officer) is not empowered to search a person for hidden weapons. The answer cannot be B, because the notification did not come through official channels, the man did not tell the special officer (security officer) that he had a weapon, and the special officer (security officer) did not observe any weapon. However, since three people have confirmed that the man has said he has a weapon and is threatening to use it, this is pretty clearly an emergency situation that calls for action. Therefore, the answer is C.

1. GENERAL RULE: A special officer (security officer) on duty at a certain entrance is not to leave his post unguarded at any time.
EXCEPTION: He may leave the post for a brief period if he first summons a replacement. He may also leave if it is necessary for him to take prompt emergency action to prevent injury to persons or property.
PROBLEM: The special officer (security officer) sees a man running down a hall with a piece of iron pipe in his hand, chasing another man who is shouting for help. By going in immediate pursuit, there is a good chance that the special officer (security officer) can stop the man with the pipe.
ACTION: The special officer (security officer) leaves his post unguarded and pursues the man.

The CORRECT answer is:

A. I   B. II   C. III   D. IV

2. GENERAL RULE: Special officers (security officers) assigned to a college campus are instructed not to arrest students for minor violations such as disorderly conduct; instead, the violation should be stopped and the incident should be reported to the college authorities, who will take disciplinary action.
EXCEPTION: A special officer (security officer) may arrest a student or take other appropriate action if failure to do so is likely to result in personal injury or property damage, or disruption of school activities, or if the incident involves serious criminal behavior.
PROBLEM: A special officer (security officer) is on duty in a college building where evening classes are being held. He is told that two students are causing a disturbance in a classroom. He arrives and finds that a fist fight is in progress and the classroom is in an uproar. The special officer (security officer) separates the two students who are fighting and takes them out of the room. Both of them seem to be intoxicated. They both have valid student ID cards.
ACTION: The special officer (security officer) takes down their names and addresses for his report, then tells them to leave the building with a warning not to return this evening.

The CORRECT answer is:

A. I   B. II   C. III   D. IV

3. GENERAL RULE: A special officer (security officer) is not permitted to carry a gun while on duty.
EXCEPTION: A special officer (security officer) who disarms a person must keep the weapon in his possession for the brief period before he can turn it over to the proper authorities. A special officer (security officer) who is NOT on duty may, like any other citizen, own and carry a gun if he has a proper permit from the Police Department.
PROBLEM: A special officer (security officer) is assigned to a post where there have been a series of violent incidents in the past few days. He feels that these incidents could have been controlled much more easily if the people involved had seen that the special officer (security officer) had a gun. He has a gun at home, for which he has a valid permit.
ACTION: The special officer (security officer) brings his gun when he goes on duty. He does not plan to use it, but just show people that he has it so that they will not start any trouble.

The CORRECT answer is:

A. I B. II C. III D. IV

4. GENERAL RULE: No one except a licensed physician or someone acting directly under a physician's orders may legally administer medicine to another person.
EXCEPTION: In a first aid situation, the special officer (security officer) is allowed to help a person suffering frori a heart condition or other disease to take medicine which the person has in his possession, provided that the person is conscious and requests this assistance.
PROBLEM: A special officer (security officer) on duty at a public building is told that a man has collapsed in the elevator. When the special officer (security officer) arrives at the scene, the man is barely conscious. He cannot speak, but he points to his pocket. The special officer (security officer) finds a pill bottle that says *one capsule in ease of need*. The man nods.
ACTION: The special officer (security officer) puts one capsule in the man's hand and guides the man's hand to his mouth.

The CORRECT answer is:

A. I B. II C. III D. IV

5. GENERAL RULE: In case of a fire drill or fire alarm, special officers (security officers) on patrol in a building are to remain in their assigned areas to assist in the evacuation of persons from the building and to make sure that no one takes advantage of the situation by stealing property that is left unguarded.
EXCEPTION: Should there be an actual fire, special officers (security officers) will follow whatever instructions are given by the firefighters or police officers who arrive on the scene to take charge.
PROBLEM: A special officer (security officer) is on duty patroling the fifth floor of a building when a fire alarm sounds. The fire is in a supply closet at one end of the fifth floor. All personnel have been evacuated from the floor. Neither police nor firemen have yet shown up.
ACTION: The special officer (security officer) stays on the fifth floor at a safe distance from the supply closet.

The CORRECT answer is:

A. I B. II C. III D. IV

KEY (CORRECT ANSWERS)

1. B
2. A
3. D
4. B
5. A

EXAMINATION SECTION
TEST 1

DIRECTIONS: Each question or incomplete statement is followed by several suggested answers or completions. Select the one that BEST answers the question or completes the statement. *PRINT THE LETTER OF THE CORRECT ANSWER IN THE SPACE AT THE RIGHT.*

1. Which of the following is the LEAST important factor to consider in surveying the physical layout of a building for traffic flow?

    A. Location of windows
    B. Number of entrances
    C. Number of exits
    D. Location of first aid rooms

2. The major purpose of any security program in a large organization is to prevent unlawful acts.
   If adequate patrol coverage is provided at a given location, it is MOST likely that

    A. crimes will not be committed
    B. undesirables will not enter the building
    C. unlawful acts will increase in the long run
    D. there will be less opportunity to commit a crime

3. The MOST frequent cause of fires in public facilities is

    A. incinerators
    B. vandalism
    C. electrical sources
    D. smoking on the job

4. After bomb threats are received, it is sometimes necessary to evacuate a facility. How long BEFORE the threatened time of explosion should a facility be evacuated?
   At least _____ minutes.

    A. 15   B. 25   C. 50   D. 60

5. Once a facility is evacuated because of a bomb threat, how much time should pass before the public and employees are allowed to enter the building?
   _____ minutes.

    A. 10   B. 20   C. 40   D. 60

6. Of the following locations in public buildings, the one which is the LEAST likely place for bombs to be planted is in

    A. storerooms
    B. bathrooms
    C. cafeterias
    D. waste receptacles

7. The one of the following that is the surest means of establishing positive identification of someone entering a facility is by

    A. personal recognition
    B. I.D. badge
    C. social security card
    D. driver's license

21

8. The one of the following which most probably would NOT be included in a police record report concerning an incident at a facility is the

   A. name of complainant or injured party
   B. name of the investigating officer
   C. statement of each witness
   D. religion of complainant or injured party

9. Preventing trouble is one of the primary concerns of special officers.
   When dealing with unruly groups of people who threaten to become violent, which of the following is a measure which should NOT be taken?

   A. Maintain close surveillance of such groups
   B. Try to contact the leaders of the group regardless of their militancy
   C. Keep the officer force alerted
   D. Have the officer force deal aggressively with provocations

10. Of the following, the MOST important factor to consider in the deployment of officers dealing with a client population is the officers' ability to

    A. remain calm   B. look stern
    C. evaluate personality D. take a firm stand

11. Assume that an offender is struggling with a group of officers who are trying to arrest him.
    What force, if any, can be used to overcome this resistance?

    A. The amount of force acceptable to the public
    B. The amount of force necessary to restrain the offender and protect the officers
    C. Any amount of force that is acceptable to the officers at the scene
    D. No force may be used until the police arrive

12. Assume that a fire is discovered at your work location. The one of the following actions which would be INAPPROPRIATE for you to take is to

    A. notify the telephone operator
    B. station a reliable person at the entrance
    C. open all windows and doors in the area
    D. start evacuating the area

13. If a person has an object caught in his throat or air passage but is breathing adequately, which one of the following should you do?

    A. Probe for the object
    B. Force him to drink water
    C. Lay him over your arm and slap him between the shoulder blades
    D. Allow him to cough and to assume the position he finds most comfortable

14. The one of the following methods which should NOT be used to report a fire is to

    A. call 911
    B. pull the handle in the red box on the street corner
    C. call the fire department county numbers listed in each county directory
    D. call 411

15. Assume that an officer, alone in a building at night, smells the strong odor of cooking or heating gas. In addition to airing the building and making sure that he is not overcome, it would be BEST for the officer to call

   A. his superior at his home and ask for instructions
   B. for a plumber from the department of public works
   C. 911 for police and fire help
   D. the emergency number at Con Edison

15.____

16. Of the following situations, the one that is MOST dangerous for an officer is when he

   A. investigates suspicious persons and circumstances
   B. finds a burglary in progress or pursues burglary suspects
   C. attempts an arrest or finds a robbery in progress
   D. patrols on the overnight shift

16.____

17. An officer on security patrol generally should spend MOST of his time

   A. checking doors and locks
   B. helping the public and answering questions
   C. chasing criminals and looking for clues
   D. writing reports on unusual incidents

17.____

18. The one of the following that is an ACCEPTABLE way to arrest a person is to

   A. tell him to report to the nearest police precinct
   B. send a summons to his permanent address
   C. tell him in person that he is under arrest
   D. show him handcuffs and ask him to come along

18.____

19. A carbon dioxide fire extinguisher is BEST suited for extinguishing _____ fires.

   A. paper   B. rag   C. rubbish   D. grease

19.____

20. A pressurized water or soda-acid fire extinguisher is BEST suited for extinguishing _____ fires.

   A. wood   B. gasoline
   C. electrical   D. magnesium

20.____

21. The one of the following statements that does NOT apply to the use of handcuffs is that they

   A. are used as temporary restraining devices
   B. eliminate the need for vigilance
   C. cannot be opened without keys
   D. are used to secure a violent person

21.____

22. The one of the following that is GENERALLY a crime against the person is

   A. trespass   B. burglary   C. robbery   D. arson

22.____

23. Of the following, the SAFEST way of escape from an office in a burning building is generally the

    A. stairway
    B. rooftop
    C. passenger elevator
    D. freight elevator

24. In attempting to control a possible riot situation, an officer pushed his way into a crowd gathered outside the building and tried to cause confusion by arguing with members of the group.
    This procedure NORMALLY is considered

    A. *desirable;* any violence that occurs will remain outside the building
    B. *desirable;* the crowd will break into smaller groups and disperse
    C. *undesirable;* to maintain control of the situation, the officer must not become part of the crowd
    D. *undesirable;* the supervisor should stay clear of the scene

25. Which one of the following is MOST effective in making officers more safety-minded?

    A. Maintaining an up-to-date library of the latest safety literature
    B. Reading daily safety bulletins at roll-call
    C. Holding informal group safety meetings periodically
    D. Offering prizes for good safety slogans and displays

KEY (CORRECT ANSWERS)

1.	A	11.	B
2.	D	12.	C
3.	C	13.	D
4.	A	14.	D
5.	D	15.	D
6.	C	16.	C
7.	A	17.	A
8.	D	18.	C
9.	D	19.	D
10.	A	20.	A

21.	B
22.	C
23.	A
24.	C
25.	C

TEST 2

DIRECTIONS: Each question or incomplete statement is followed by several suggested answers or completions. Select the one that BEST answers the question or completes the statement. *PRINT THE LETTER OF THE CORRECT ANSWER IN THE SPACE AT THE RIGHT.*

1. Assume that an angry crowd of some 75 to 100 people has built up in one of the hallways of a center and that only one superior officer and two subordinate officers are on duty in the building. A glass panel in one of the stairway doors has just been broken under the pressure of the crowd and a bench has been hurled down a flight of stairs. The one of the following actions that the superior officer SHOULD take in this situation is to

    A. push his way into the crowd and try to reason with them
    B. order the two other officers to try to quiet the crowd
    C. call the police on 911 and meet them outside the building
    D. do nothing at this point in order to avoid a riot

2. One of the duties and responsibilities of a supervisor is to test the knowledge of the officers concerning their post conditions.
   This should be done if the officer's assignment is

    A. fixed only
    B. roving only
    C. roving only in a troublesome spot
    D. either fixed or roving

3. An officer discovers early one morning that an office in the building he guards has been burglarized.
   Of the following, it is important for the officer to FIRST

    A. go through the building and look for suspects
    B. call the police and protect the area and whatever evidence exists until they arrive
    C. allow people into their offices as they come to work
    D. examine, sort, and handle all evidence before the police get there

4. Assume that two officers are interrogating one suspect. How should these officers position themselves during the interrogation?

    A. One officer should stand on either side of the suspect.
    B. One officer should stand to the right of the suspect, and the other officer should stand behind the suspect.
    C. Both officers should stand to the right of the suspect.
    D. One officer should stand to the right of the suspect, and the other officer should stand in front of the suspect.

5. A witness who takes an oath to testify truly and who states as true any matter which he knows to be false is guilty of

    A. perjury   B. libel   C. slander   D. fraud

6. An officer checking a substance suspected of containing narcotics should GENERALLY

   A. taste it in small amounts
   B. send it to a laboratory for analysis
   C. smell it for its distinctive odor
   D. examine it for its unusual texture

7. A certain center is situated in an area where frequent outbreaks of hostilities seem to be focused on the center itself.
Which of the following BEST explains why the center may be a target for hostile acts?
It

   A. serves community needs
   B. represents governmental authority
   C. represents all ethnic groups
   D. serves as a neutral battlefield

8. An officer often deals with people who might be addicted to drugs.
The one of the following symptoms which is NOT generally an indication of drug addiction is

   A. dilation of the eye pupils
   B. frequent yawning and sneezing
   C. a deep, rasping cough
   D. continual itching of the arms and legs

9. In emergency situations, panic will MOST probably occur when people are

   A. unexpectedly confronted with a terrorizing condition from which there appears to be no escape
   B. angry and violent
   C. anxious about circumstances which are not obvious, easily visible or within the immediate area
   D. familiar with the effects of the emergency

10. The one of the following actions on the part of a person that would NOT be considered *resisting arrest* is

    A. retreating and running away
    B. saying, *You can't arrest me*
    C. pushing the officer aside
    D. pulling away from an officer's grasp

11. Which of the following items would NOT be considered an APPROPRIATE item of uniform for an officer to wear while on duty?

    A. Reefer type overcoat
    B. Leather laced shoes with flat soles
    C. White socks
    D. Cap cover with cap device displayed

12. What can happen to an officer if the leather thong on his night stick is NOT twisted correctly?
    The
    A. baton may be taken out of the officer's hand
    B. officer's wrist may be broken
    C. leather will tear more easily
    D. officer's arm may be injured

13. The one of the following kinds of information which SHOULD be included in the log book is
    A. any important matter of police information
    B. an item noted in Standard Operating Procedures only
    C. everything of general interest
    D. a crime or offense only

14. While on patrol at your work location, you receive a call that an assault has taken place. Upon your arrival at the scene, the victim, who has severe lacerations, informs you that the assailant ran into a nearby basement.
    After apprehending the suspect, the type of search you should conduct is a _____ search.
    A. wall   B. frisk   C. body   D. strip

15. A tactical force is valuable in MOST emergency situations PRIMARILY because of its
    A. location   B. morale
    C. flexibility   D. size

16. An officer should be encouraged to talk easily and frankly when he is dealing with his superior.
    In order to encourage such free communication, it would be MOST appropriate for a superior to behave in a(n)
    A. *sincere* manner; assure the officer that you will deal with him honestly and openly
    B. *official* manner; you are a superior officer and must always act formally with subordinates
    C. *investigative* manner; you must probe and question to get to a basis of trust
    D. *unemotional* manner; the officer's emotions and background should play no part in your dealings with him

17. Research findings show that an increase in free communication within an agency GENERALLY results in which one of the following?
    A. Improved morale and productivity
    B. Increased promotional opportunities
    C. An increase in authority
    D. A spirit of honesty

18. Assume that you are a superior officer and your superiors have given you a new arrest procedure to be followed. Before passing this information on to your subordinates, the one of the following actions that you should take FIRST is to

    A. ask your superiors to send out a memorandum to the entire staff
    B. clarify the procedure in your own mind
    C. set up a training course to provide instructions on the new procedure
    D. write a memorandum to your subordinates

19. Communication is necessary for an organization to be effective.
    The one of the following which is LEAST important for most communication systems is that

    A. messages are sent quickly and directly to the person who needs them to operate
    B. information should be conveyed understandably and accurately
    C. the method used to transmit information should be kept secret so that security can be maintained
    D. senders of messages must know how their messages were received and acted upon

20. Which one of the following is the CHIEF advantage of listening willingly to subordinate officers and encouraging them to talk freely and honestly?
    It

    A. reveals to superiors the degree to which ideas that are passed down are accepted by subordinates
    B. reduces the participation of subordinates in the operation of the department
    C. encourages officers to try for promotion
    D. enables officers to learn about security leaks on the part of officials

21. A superior may be informed through either oral or written reports.
    Which one of the following is an ADVANTAGE of using oral reports?

    A. There is no need for a formal record of the report.
    B. An exact duplicate of the report is not easily transmitted to others.
    C. A good oral report requires little time for preparation.
    D. An oral report involves two-way communication between a subordinate and his superior.

22. Of the following, the MOST important reason why officers should communicate effectively with the public is to

    A. improve the public's understanding of information that is important for them to know
    B. establish a friendly relationship
    C. obtain information about the kinds of people who come to the center
    D. convince the public that services are adequate

23. Officers should generally NOT use phrases like *too hard, too easy,* and *a lot* principally because such phrases

    A. may be offensive to some minority groups
    B. are too informal

C. mean different things to different people
D. are difficult to remember

24. The ability to communicate clearly and concisely is an important element in effective leadership.
Which of the following statements about oral and written communication is GENERALLY true?

   A. Oral communication is more time-consuming.
   B. Written communication is more likely to be misinterpreted.
   C. Oral communication is useful only in emergencies.
   D. Written communication is useful mainly when giving information to fewer than twenty people.

24._____

25. Rumors can often have harmful and disruptive effects on an organization.
Which one of the following is the BEST way to prevent rumors from becoming a problem?

   A. Refuse to act on rumors, thereby making them less believable
   B. Increase the amount of information passed along by the *grapevine*
   C. Distribute as much factual information as possible
   D. Provide training in report writing

25._____

KEY (CORRECT ANSWERS)

1.	C	11.	C
2.	D	12.	A
3.	B	13.	A
4.	B	14.	A
5.	A	15.	C
6.	B	16.	A
7.	B	17.	A
8.	C	18.	B
9.	A	19.	C
10.	B	20.	A

21. D
22. A
23. C
24. B
25. C

EXAMINATION SECTION
TEST 1

DIRECTIONS: Each question or incomplete statement is followed by several suggested answers or completions. Select the one that BEST answers the question or completes the statement. *PRINT THE LETTER OF THE CORRECT ANSWER IN THE SPACE AT THE RIGHT.*

Questions 1-4.

DIRECTIONS: Questions 1 through 4 are based on the picture entitled *Contents of a Woman's Handbag*. Assume that all of the contents are shown in the picture.

<u>CONTENTS OF A WOMAN'S HANDBAG</u>

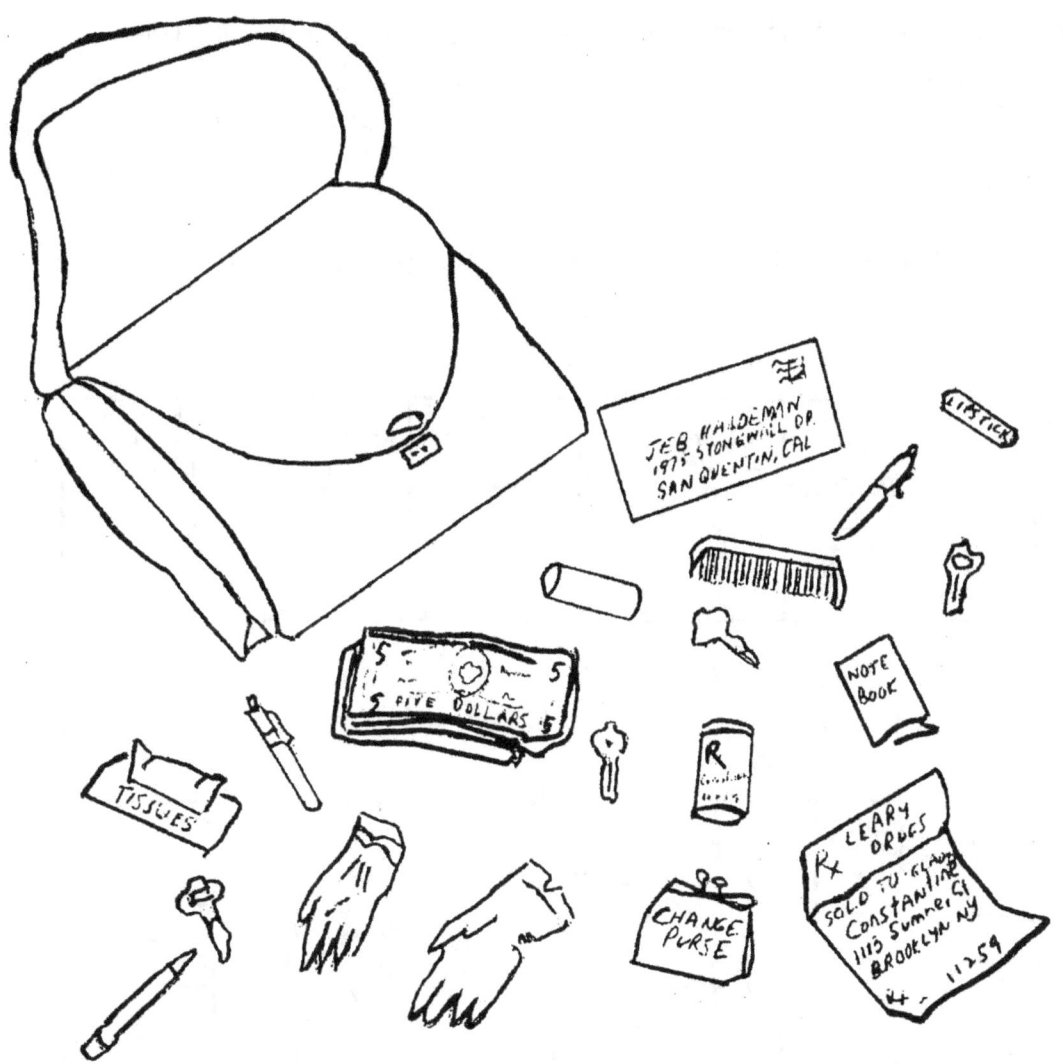

1. Where does Gladys Constantine live?

    A. Chalmers Street in Manhattan
    B. Summer Street in Manhattan
    C. Summer Street in Brooklyn
    D. Chalmers Street in Brooklyn

2. How many keys were in the handbag?

    A. 2   B. 3   C. 4   D. 5

3. How much money was in the handbag? _____ dollar(s).

    A. Exactly five   B. More than five
    C. Exactly ten   D. Less than one

4. The sales slip found in the handbag shows the purchase of which of the following?

    A. The handbag   B. Lipstick
    C. Tissues   D. Prescription medicine

Questions 5-8.

DIRECTIONS: Questions 5 through 8 are based on the floor plan below.

FLOOR PLAN

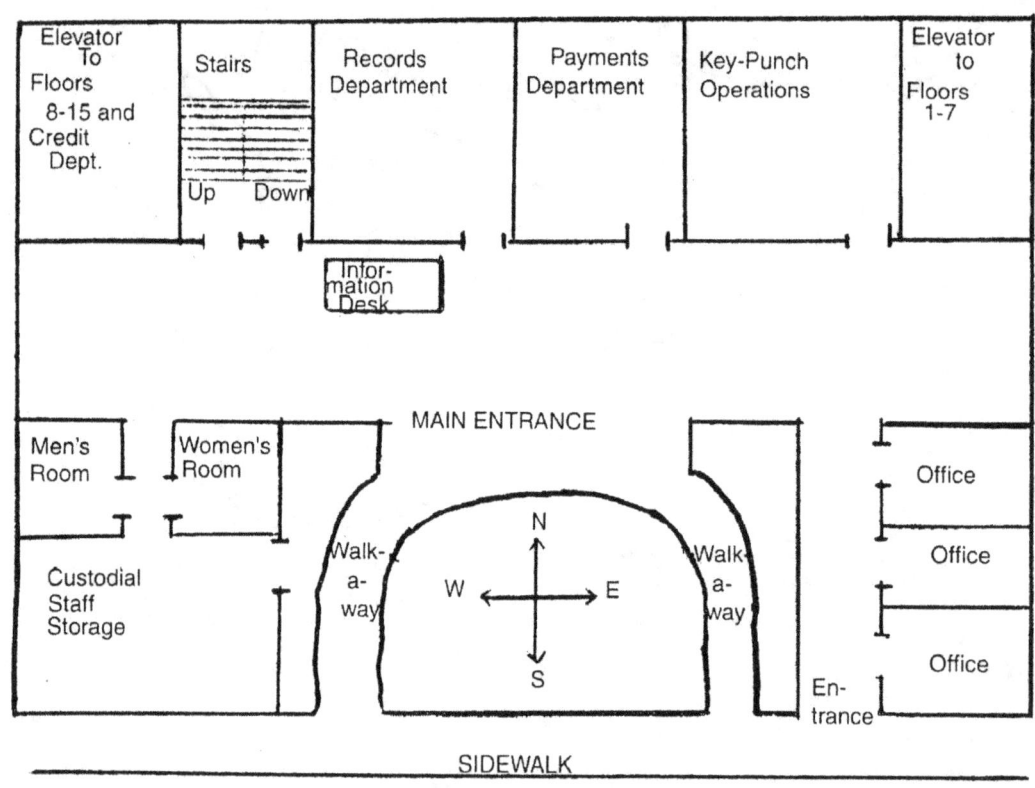

5. A special officer (security officer) on duty at the main entrance must be aware of other outside entrances to his area of the building. These unguarded entrances are usually kept locked, but they are important in case of fire or other emergency.
   Besides the main entrance, how many OTHER entrances shown on the floor plan directly face Forty-ninth Street?
   _____ other entrances.

   A. No B. One C. Two D. Three

6. A person who arrives at the main entrance and asks to be directed to the Credit Department SHOULD be told to

   A. take the elevator on the left
   B. take the elevator on the right
   C. go to a different entrance
   D. go up the stairs on the left

7. On the east side of the entrance can be found

   A. a storage room   B. offices
   C. toilets   D. stairs

8. The space DIRECTLY BEHIND the Information Desk in the floor plan is occupied by

   A. up and down stairs   B. key punch operations
   C. toilets   D. the records department

Questions 9-12.

DIRECTIONS: Answer Questions 9 to 12 on the basis of the information given in the passage below.

The public often believes that the main job of a uniformed officer is to enforce laws by simply arresting people. In reality, however, many of the situations that an officer deals with do not call for the use of his arrest power. In the first place, an officer spends much of his time preventing crimes from happening, by spotting potential violations or suspicious behavior and taking action to prevent illegal acts. In the second place, many of the situations in which officers are called on for assistance involve elements like personal arguments, husband-wife quarrels, noisy juveniles, or mentally disturbed persons. The majority of these problems do not result in arrests and convictions, and often they do not even involve illegal behavior. In the third place, even in situations where there seems to be good reason to make an arrest, an officer may have to exercise very good judgment. There are times when making an arrest too soon could touch off a riot, or could result in the detention of a minor offender while major offenders escaped, or could cut short the gathering of necessary on-the-scene evidence.

9. The above passage IMPLIES that most citizens

   A. will start to riot if they see an arrest being made
   B. appreciate the work that law enforcement officers do
   C. do not realize that making arrests is only a small part of law enforcement
   D. never call for assistance unless they are involved in a personal argument or a husband-wife quarrel

10. According to the passage, one way in which law enforcement officers can prevent crimes from happening is by

   A. arresting suspicious characters
   B. letting minor offenders go free
   C. taking action on potential violations
   D. refusing to get involved in husband-wife fights

11. According to the passage, which of the following statements is NOT true of situations involving mentally disturbed persons?

   A. It is a waste of time to call on law enforcement officers for assistance in such situations.
   B. Such situations may not involve illegal behavior
   C. Such situations often do not result in arrests.
   D. Citizens often turn to law enforcement officers for help in such situations.

12. The last sentence in the passage mentions *detention of minor offenders.*
   Of the following, which BEST explains the meaning of the word *detention* as used here?

   A. Sentencing someone
   B. Indicting someone
   C. Calling someone before a grand jury
   D. Arresting someone

Questions 13-28.

DIRECTIONS: In answering Questions 13 through 28, assume that *you* means a special officer (security officer) on duty. Your basic responsibilities are safeguarding people and property and maintaining order in the area to which you are assigned. You are in uniform, and you are not armed. You keep in touch with your supervisory station either by telephone or by a two-way radio (walkie-talkie).

13. It is a general rule that if the security alarm goes off showing that someone has made an unlawful entrance into a building, no officer responsible for security shall proceed to investigate alone. Each officer must be accompanied by at least one other officer.
   Of the following, which is the MOST probable reason for this rule?

   A. It is dangerous for an officer to investigate such a situation alone.
   B. The intruder might try to bribe an officer to let him go.
   C. One officer may be inexperienced and needs an experienced partner.
   D. Two officers are better than one officer in writing a report of the investigation.

14. You are on weekend duty on the main floor of a public building. The building is closed to the public on weekends, but some employees are sometimes asked to work weekends. You have been instructed to use cautious good judgment in opening the door for such persons.
   Of the following, which one MOST clearly shows the poorest judgment?

A. Admitting an employee who is personally known to you without asking to see any identification except the permit slip signed by the employee's supervisor
B. Refusing to admit someone whom you do not recognize but who claims left his identification at home
C. Admitting to the building only those who can give a detailed description of their weekend work duties
D. Leaving the entrance door locked for a while to make regulation security checks of other areas in the building with the result that no one can either enter or leave during these periods

15. You are on duty at a public building. An office employee tells you that she left her purse in her desk when she went out to lunch, and she has just discovered that it is gone. She has been back from lunch for half an hour and has not left her desk during this period. What should you do FIRST?

    A. Warn all security personnel to stop any suspicious-looking person who is seen with a purse
    B. Ask for a description of the purse
    C. Call the Lost and Found and ask if a purse has been turned in
    D. Obtain statements from any employees who were in the office during the lunch hour

16. You are patrolling your assigned area in a public building. You hear a sudden crash and the sound of running footsteps. You investigate and find that someone has forced open a locked entrance to the building. What is the FIRST thing you should do?

    A. Close the door and try to fix the lock so that no one else can get in
    B. Use your two-way radio to report the emergency and summon help
    C. Chase after the person whose running footsteps you heard
    D. Go immediately to your base office and make out a brief written report

17. You and another special officer (security officer) are on duty in the main waiting area at a welfare center. A caseworker calls both of you over and whispers that one of the clients, Richard Roe, may be carrying a gun. Of the following, what is the BEST action for both of you to take?

    A. You should approach the man, one on each side, and one of you should say loudly and clearly, "Richard Roe, you are under arrest."
    B. Both of you should ask the man to go with you to a private room, and then find out if he is carrying a gun
    C. Both of you should grab him, handcuff him, and take him to the nearest precinct station house
    D. Both of you should watch him carefully but not do anything unless he actually pulls a gun

18. You are on duty at a welfare center. You are told that a caseworker is being threatened by a man with a knife. You go immediately to the scene, and you find the caseworker lying on the floor with blood spurting from a wound in his arm. You do not know who the attacker is. What should you do FIRST?

    A. Ask the caseworker for a description of the attacker so that you can set out in pursuit and try to catch him
    B. Take down the names and addresses of any witnesses to the incident

C. Give first aid to the caseworker, if you can, and immediately call for an ambulance
D. Search the people standing around in the room for the knife

19. As a special officer (security officer), you have been patrolling a special section of a hospital building for a week. Smoking is not allowed in this section because the oxygen tanks in use here could easily explode. However, you have observed that some employees sneak into the linen-supply room in this section in order to smoke without anybody seeing them.
Of the following, which is the BEST way for you to deal with this situation?

    A. Whenever you catch anyone smoking, call his supervisor immediately
    B. Request the Building Superintendent to put a padlock on the door of the linen-supply room
    C. Ignore the smoking because you do not want to get a reputation for interfering in the private affairs of other employees
    D. Report the situation to your supervisor and follow his instructions

19.____

20. You are on duty at a hospital. You have been assigned to guard the main door, and you are responsible for remaining at your post until relieved. On one of the wards for which you are not responsible, there is a patient who was wounded in a street fight. This patient is under arrest for killing another man in this fight, and he is supposed to be under round-the-clock police guard. A nurse tells you that one of the police officers assigned to guard the patient has suddenly taken ill and has to periodically leave his post to go to the washroom. The nurse is worried because she thinks the patient might try to escape.
Of the following, which is the BEST action for you to take?

    A. Tell the nurse to call you whenever the police officer leaves his post so that you can keep an eye on the patient while the officer is gone
    B. Assume that the police officer probably knows his job, and that there is no reason for you to worry
    C. Alert your supervisor to the nurse's report
    D. Warn the police officer that the nurse has been talking about him

20.____

21. You are on night duty at a hospital where you are responsible for patrolling a large section of the main building. Your supervisor tells you that there have been several nighttime thefts from a supply room in your section and asks you to be especially alert for suspicious activity near this supply room.
Of the following, which is the MOST reasonable way to carry out your supervisor's direction?

    A. Check the supply room regularly at half-hour intervals
    B. Make frequent checks of the supply room at irregular intervals
    C. Station yourself by the door of the supply room and stay at this post all night
    D. Find a hidden spot from which you can watch the supply room and stay there all night

21.____

22. You are on duty at a vehicle entrance to a hospital. Parking space on the hospital grounds is strictly limited, and no one is ever allowed to park there unless they have an official parking permit. You have just stopped a driver who does not have a parking permit, but he explains that
he is a doctor and he has a patient in the hospital. What should you do?

22.____

A. Let him park since he has explained that he is a doctor
B. Ask in a friendly way, *"Can I check your identification?"*
C. Call the Information Desk to make sure there is such a patient in the hospital
D. Tell the driver politely but firmly that he will have to park somewhere else

23. You are on duty at a public building. A man was just mugged on a stairway. The mugger took the man's wallet and started to run down the stairs but tripped and fell. Now the mugger is lying unconscious at the bottom of the stairs and bleeding from the mouth.
The FIRST thing you should do is to

    A. search him to see if he is carrying any other stolen property
    B. pick him up and carry him away from the stairs
    C. try and revive him for questioning
    D. put in a call for an ambulance and police assistance

24. After someone breaks into an employee's locker at a public building, you interview the employee to determine what is missing from the locker. The employee becomes hysterical and asks why you are *wasting time with all these questions* instead of going after the thief.
The MOST reasonable thing for you to do is

    A. tell the employee that it is very important to have an accurate description of the missing articles
    B. quietly tell the employee to calm down and stop interfering with your work
    C. explain to the employee that you are only doing what you were told to do and that you don't make the rules
    D. assure the employee that there are a lot of people working on the case and that someone else is probably arresting the thief right now

25. You are on duty at a public building. An employee reports that a man has just held her up and taken her money. The employee says that the man was about 25 years old, with short blond hair and a pale complexion and was wearing blue jeans.
Of the following additional facts, which one would probably be MOST valuable to officers searching the building for the suspect?

    A. The man was wearing dark glasses.
    B. He had on a green jacket.
    C. He was about 5 feet 8 inches tall.
    D. His hands and fingernails were very dirty.

26. When the fire alarm goes off, it is your job as a special officer (security officer) to see that all employees leave the building quickly by the correct exits. A fire alarm has just sounded, and you are checking the offices on one of the floors. A supervisor in one office tells you, *"This is probably just another fire drill. I've sent my office staff out, but I don't want to stop my own work."*
What should you do?

    A. Insist politely but firmly that the supervisor must obey the fire rules.
    B. Tell the supervisor that it is all right this time but that the rules must be followed in the future.
    C. Tell the supervisor that he is under arrest.
    D. Allow the supervisor to do as he sees fit since he is in charge of his own office.

27. You are on duty on the main floor of a public building. You have been informed that a briefcase has just been stolen from an office on the tenth floor. You see a man getting off the elevator with a briefcase that matches the description of the one that was stolen.
What is the FIRST action you should take?

   A. Arrest the man and take him to the nearest public station
   B. Stop the man and say politely that you want to take a look at the briefcase
   C. Take the briefcase from the man and tell him that he cannot have it back unless he can prove that it is his
   D. Do not stop the man but note down his description and the exact time he got off the elevator

28. You are on duty at a welfare center. You have been told that two clients are arguing with a caseworker and making loud threats. You go to the scene, but the caseworker tells you that everything is now under control. The two clients, who are both mean-looking characters, are still there but seem to be acting normally.
What SHOULD you do?

   A. Apologize for having made a mistake and go away.
   B. Arrest the two men for having caused a disturbance.
   C. Insist on standing by until the interview is over, then escort the two men from the building.
   D. Leave the immediate scene but watch for any further developments.

29. You are on duty at a welfare center. A client comes up to you and says that two men just threatened him with a knife and made him give them his money. The client has alcohol on his breath and he is shabbily dressed. He points out the two men he says took the money.
Of the following, which is the BEST action to take?

   A. Arrest the two men on the client's complaint.
   B. Ignore the client's complaint since he doesn't look as if he could have had any money.
   C. Suggest to the client that he may be imagining things.
   D. Investigate and find out what happened.

Questions 30-35.

DIRECTIONS: Answer Questions 30 through 35 on the basis of the information given in the passage below. Assume that all questions refer to the same state described in the passage.

The courts and the police consider an "offense" as any conduct that is punishable by a fine or imprisonment. Such offenses include many kinds of acts - from behavior that is merely annoying, like throwing a noisy party that keeps everyone awake, all the way up to violent acts like murder. The law classifies offenses according to the penalties that are provided for them. In one state, minor offenses are called "violations." A violation is punishable by a fine of not more than $250 or imprisonment of not more than. 15 days, or both. The annoying behavior mentioned above is an example of a violation. More serious offenses are classified as "crimes." Crimes are classified by the kind of penalty that is provided. A "misdemeanor" is a crime that is punishable by a fine of not more than $1,000 or by imprisonment of not more than one year, or both. Examples of misdemeanors include stealing something with a value of $100 or less, turning in a false alarm, or illegally possessing less than 1/8 of an ounce of a dangerous drug. A "felony" is a criminal offense punishable by imprisonment of more than one year. Murder is clearly a felony.

30. According to the above passage, any act that is punishable by imprisonment or by a fine is called a(n)

    A. offense   B. violation   C. crime   D. felony

31. According to the above passage, which of the following is classified as a crime?

    A. Offense punishable by 15 days imprisonment
    B. Minor offense
    C. Violation
    D. Misdemeanor

32. According to the above passage, if a person guilty of burglary can receive a prison sentence of 7 years or more, burglary would be classified as a

    A. violation   B. misdemeanor
    C. felony   D. violent act

33. According to the above passage, two offenses that would BOTH be classified as misdemeanors are

    A. making unreasonable noise and stealing a $90 bicycle
    B. stealing a $75 radio and possessing 1/16 of an ounce of heroin
    C. holding up a bank and possessing 1/4 of a pound of marijuana
    D. falsely reporting a fire and illegally double-parking

34. The above passage says that offenses are classified according to the penalties provided for them.
    On the basis of clues in the passage, who probably decides what the maximum penalties should be for the different kinds of offenses?

    A. The State lawmakers   B. The City police
    C. The Mayor   D. Officials in Washington, B.C.

35. Of the following, which BEST describes the subject matter of the passage?

    A. How society deals with criminals
    B. How offenses are classified
    C. Three types of criminal behavior
    D. The police approach to offenders

KEY (CORRECT ANSWERS)

1. C
2. C
3. B
4. D
5. B

6. A
7. B
8. D
9. C
10. C

11. A
12. D
13. A
14. C
15. B

16. B
17. B
18. C
19. D
20. C

21. B
22. D
23. D
24. A
25. C

26. A
27. B
28. D
29. D
30. A

31. D
32. C
33. B
34. A
35. B

TEST 2

DIRECTIONS: Each question or incomplete statement is followed by several suggested answers or completions. Select the one that BEST answers the question or completes the statement. *PRINT THE LETTER OF THE CORRECT ANSWER IN THE SPACE AT THE RIGHT.*

Questions 1-5.

DIRECTIONS: Questions 1 through 5 are based on the drawing below showing a view of a waiting area in a public building.

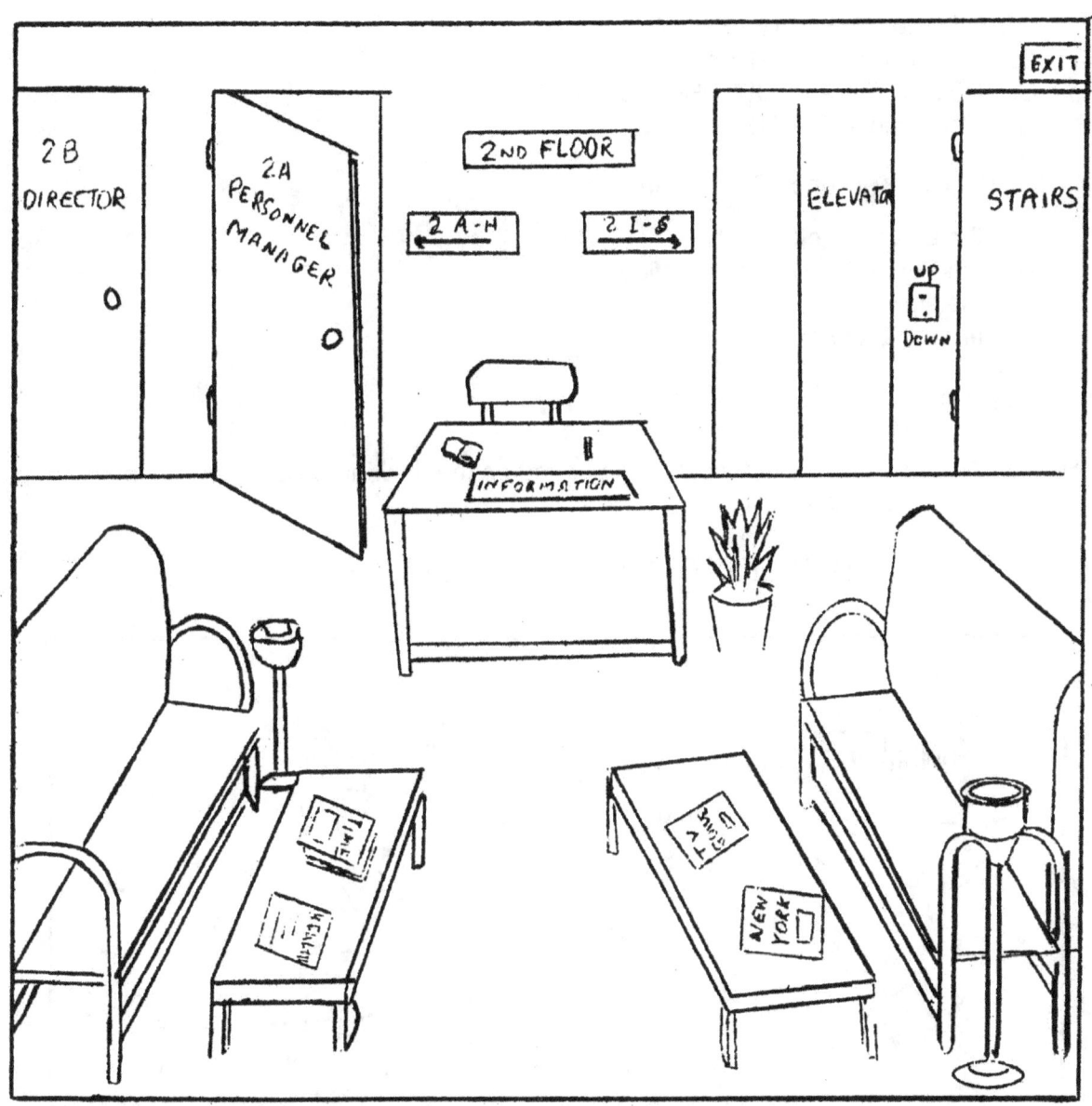

1. A desk is shown in the drawing. Which of the following is on the desk? A(n)   1.____

     A. plant   B. telephone
     C. In-Out file   D. *Information* sign

41

2. On which floor is the waiting area?

   A. Basement
   B. Main floor
   C. Second floor
   D. Third floor

3. The door IMMEDIATELY TO THE RIGHT of the desk is a(n)

   A. door to the Personnel Office
   B. elevator door
   C. door to another corridor
   D. door to the stairs

4. Among the magazines on the tables in the waiting area are

   A. TIME and NEWSWEEK
   B. READER'S DIGEST and T.V. GUIDE
   C. NEW YORK and READER'S DIGEST
   D. TIME and T.V. GUIDE

5. One door is partly open. This is the door to

   A. the Director's office
   B. the Personnel Manager's office
   C. the stairs
   D. an unmarked office

Questions 6-9.

DIRECTIONS: Questions 6 through 9 are based on the drawing below showing the contents of a male suspect's pockets.

CONTENTS OF A MALE SUSPECT'S POCKETS

6. The suspect had a slip in his pockets showing an appointment at an out-patient clinic on   6._____

   A. February 9, 2013   B. September 2, 2013
   C. February 19, 2013   D. September 12, 2013

7. The MP3 player that was found on the suspect was made by   7._____

   A. RCA   B. GE   C. Sony   D. Zenith

8. The coins found in the suspect's pockets have a TOTAL value of   8._____

   A. 56¢   B. 77¢   C. $1.05   D. $1.26

9. All except one of the following were found in the suspect's pockets.   9._____
   Which was NOT found? A

   A. ticket stub   B. comb
   C. subway fare   D. pen

Questions 10-18

DIRECTIONS: In answering Questions 10 through 18, assume that *you* means a special officer (security officer) on duty. Your basic responsibilities are safeguarding people and property and maintaining order in the area to which you are assigned. You are in uniform, and you are not armed. You keep in touch with your supervisory station either by telephone or by a two-way radio (a walkie-talkie).

10. You are on duty at a center run by the Department of Social Services. Two teenaged   10._____
    boys are on their way out of the center. As they go past you, they look at you and laugh, and one makes a remark to you in Spanish. You do not understand Spanish, but you suspect it was a nasty remark.
    What SHOULD you do?

    A. Give the boys a lecture about showing respect for a uniform.
    B. Tell the boys that they had better stay away from the center from now on.
    C. Call for an interpreter and insist that the boy repeat the remark to the interpreter.
    D. Let the boys go on their way since they have done nothing requiring your intervention.

11. You are on duty at a shelter run by the Department of Social Services. You know that   11._____
    many of the shelter clients have drinking problems, drug problems, or mental health problems. You get a call for assistance from a caseworker who says a fight has broken out. When you arrive on the scene, you see that about a dozen clients are engaged in a free-for-all and that two or three of them have pulled knives.
    The BEST course of action is to

    A. call for additional assistance and order all bystanders away from the area
    B. jump into the center of the fighting group and try to separate the fighters
    C. pick up a heavy object and start swinging at anybody who has a knife
    D. try to find out what clients started the fight and place them under arrest

12. You have been assigned to duty at a children's shelter run by the Department of Social Services. The children range in age from 6 to 15, and many of them are at the shelter because they have no homes to go to.
    Of the following, which is the BEST attitude for you to take in dealing with these youngsters?

    A. Assume that they admire and respect anyone in uniform and that they will not usually give you much trouble
    B. Assume that they fear and distrust anyone in uniform and that they are going to give you a hard time unless you act tough
    C. Expect that many of them are going to become juvenile delinquents because of their bad backgrounds and that you should be suspicious of everything they do
    D. Expect that many of them may be emotionally upset and that you should be alert for unusual behavior

13. You are on duty outside the emergency room of a hospital. You notice that an old man has been sitting on a bench outside the room for a long time. He arrived alone, and he has not spoken to anyone at all.
    What SHOULD you do?

    A. Pay no attention to him since he is not bothering anyone.
    B. Tell him to leave since he does not seem to have any business there.
    C. Ask him if you can help him in any way.
    D. Do not speak to him, but keep an eye on him.

14. You are patrolling a section of a public building. An elderly woman carrying a heavy shopping bag asks you if you would watch the shopping bag for her while she keeps an appointment in the building.
    What SHOULD you do?

    A. Watch the shopping bag for her since her appointment probably will not take long.
    B. Refuse her request, explaining that your duties keep you on the move.
    C. Agree to her request just to be polite, but then continue your patrol after the woman is out of sight.
    D. Find a bystander who will agree to watch the shopping bag for her.

15. You are on duty at a public building. It is nearly 6:00 P.M., and most employees have left for the day.
    You see two well-dressed men carrying an office calculating machine out of the building. You SHOULD

    A. stop them and ask for an explanation
    B. follow them to see where they are going
    C. order them to put down the machine and leave the building immediately
    D. take no action since they do not look like burglars

16. You are on duty patrolling a public building. You have just tripped on the stairs and turned your ankle. The ankle hurts and is starting to swell.
    What is the BEST thing to do?

A. Take a taxi to a hospital emergency room, and from there have a hospital employee call your supervisor to explain the situation.
B. First try soaking your foot in cold water for half an hour, then go off duty if you really cannot walk at all.
C. Report the situation to your supervisor, explaining that you need prompt medical attention for your ankle.
D. Find a place where you can sit until you are due to go off duty, then have a doctor look at your ankle.

17. One of your duties as a special officer (security officer) on night patrol in a public building is to check the washrooms to see that the taps are turned off and that there are no plumbing leaks.
Of the following possible reasons for this inspection, which is probably the MOST important reason?

   A. If the floor gets wet, someone might slip and fall the next morning.
   B. A running water tap might be a sign that there is an intruder in the building.
   C. A washroom flood could leak through the ceilings and walls below and cause a lot of damage.
   D. Leaks must be reported quickly so that repairs can be scheduled as soon as possible.

17.____

18. You are on duty at a public building. A department supervisor tells you that someone has left a suspicious-looking package in the hallway on his floor. You investigate, and you hear ticking in the parcel. You think it could be a bomb.
The FIRST thing you should do is to

   A. rapidly question employees on this floor to get a description of the person who left the package
   B. write down the description of the package and the name of the department supervisor
   C. notify your security headquarters that there may be a bomb in the building and that all personnel should be evacuated
   D. pick up the package carefully and remove it from the building as quickly as you can

18.____

Questions 19-22.

DIRECTIONS: Answer Questions 19 through 22 on the basis of the Fact Situation and the Report of Arrest form below. Questions 19 through 22 ask how the report form should be filled in based on the information given in the Fact Situation.

FACT SITUATION

Jesse Stein is a special officer (security officer) who is assigned to a welfare center at 435 East Smythe Street, Brooklyn. He was on duty there Thursday morning, February 1. At 10:30 A.M., a client named Jo Ann Jones, 40 years old, arrived with her ten-year-old son, Peter. Another client, Mary Alice Wiell, 45 years old, immediately began to insult Mrs. Jones. When Mrs. Jones told her to "go away," Mrs. Wiell pulled out a long knife. The special officer (security officer) intervened and requested Mrs. Wiell to drop the knife. She would not, and he had to use necessary force to disarm her. He arrested her on charges of disorderly conduct, harassment, and possession of a dangerous weapon. Mrs. Wiell lives at 118 Heally Street,

Brooklyn, Apartment 4F, and she is unemployed. The reason for her aggressive behavior is not known.

```
┌─────────────────────────────────────────────────────────────────────────┐
│ REPORT OF ARREST                                                        │
│ 01) _____    (08) _____           │
│     (Prisoner's surname) (first) (initial)    (Precinct)                │
│ 02) _____    (09) _____           │
│     (Address)                                 (Date of arrest)          │
│                                               (Month, Day)              │
│ 03) _____ (04) _____ (05) _____   (10) _____          │
│     (Date of birth) (Age)  (Sex)              (Time of arrest)          │
│ 06) _____ (07) _____      (11) _____          │
│     (Occupation)    (Where employed)          (Place of arrest)         │
│ 12) _____       │
│     (Specific offenses)                                                 │
│ 13) _____  (14) _____                │
│     (Arresting Officer)                 (Officer's No.)                 │
└─────────────────────────────────────────────────────────────────────────┘
```

19. What entry should be made in Blank 01?

    A. Jo Ann Jones   B. Jones, Jo Ann
    C. Mary Wiell   D. Wiell, Mary A.

20. Which of the following should be entered in Blank 04?

    A. 40   B. 40's   C. 45   D. Middle-aged

21. Which of the following should be entered in Blank 09?

    A. Wednesday, February 1, 10:30 A.M.
    B. February 1
    C. Thursday morning, February 2
    D. Morning, February 4

22. Of the following, which would be the BEST entry to make in Blank 11?

    A. Really Street Welfare Center
    B. Brooklyn
    C. 435 E. Smythe St., Brooklyn
    D. 118 Heally St., Apt. 4F

Questions 23-27.

DIRECTIONS: Answer Questions 23 through 27 on the basis of the information given in the Report of Loss or Theft that appears below.

```
REPORT OF LOSS OR THEFT          Date: 12/4    Time: 9:15 a.m.
Complaint made by:  Richard Aldridge         [ ] Owner
                    306 S. Walter St.        [x] Other - explain:
                                             Head of Accty. Dept.
Type of property:  Computer                  Value: $550.00
Description: Dell
Location: 768 N Margin Ave., Accounting Dept., 3rd Floor
Time: Overnight 12/3 - 12/4
Circumstances: Mr. Aldridge reports he arrived at work 8:45 A.M.,
found office door open and machine missing. Nothing else reported
missing. I investigated and found signs of forced entry: door lock
was broken.          Signature of Reporting Officer: B.L. Ramirez
Notify:
    [ ] Building & Grounds Office, 768 N. Margin Ave.
    [ ] Lost Property Office, 110 Brand Ave.
    [x] Security Office, 703 N. Wide Street
```

23. The person who made this complaint is

    A. a secretary   B. a security officer
    C. Richard Aldridge   D. B.L. Ramirez

24. The report concerns a computer that has been

    A. lost   B. damaged   C. stolen   D. sold

25. The person who took the computer probably entered the office through

    A. a door   B. a window   C. the roof   D. the basement

26. When did the head of the Accounting Department first notice that the computer was missing?

    A. December 4 at 9:15 A.M.   B. December 4 at 8:45 A.M.
    C. The night of December 3   D. The night of December 4

27. The event described in the report took place at

    A. 306 South Walter Street   B. 768 North Margin Avenue
    C. 110 Brand Avenue   D. 703 North Wide Street

Questions 28-33.

DIRECTIONS: Answer Questions 28 through 33 on the basis of the instructions, the code, and the sample question given below.

Assume that a special officer (security officer) at a certain location is equipped with a two-way radio to keep him in constant touch with his security headquarters. Radio messages and replies are given in code form, as follows:

Radio Code for Situation	J	P	M	F	B
Radio Code for Action to be Taken	o	r	a	z	q
Radio Response for Action Being Taken	1	2	3	4	5

Assume that each of the above capital letters is the radio code for a particular type of situation, that the small letter below each capital letter is the radio code for the action a special officer (security officer) is directed to take, and that the number directly below each small letter is the radio response a special officer (security officer) should make to indicate what action was actually taken.

In each of the following Questions 28 through 33, the code letter for the action directed (Column 2) and the code number for the action taken (Column 3) should correspond to the capital letters in Column 1.

If only Column 2 is different from Column 1, mark your answer A.

If only Column 3 is different from Column 1, mark your answer B.

If both Column 2 and Column 3 are different from Column 1, mark your answer C.

If both Columns 2 and 3 are the same as Column 1, mark your answer D.

SAMPLE QUESTION

Column 1	Column 2	Column 3
JPFMB	orzaq	12453

The code letters in Column 2 are correct, but the numbers 53 in Column 3 should be 35. Therefore, the answer is B.

	Column 1	Column 2	Column 3	
28.	PBFJM	rqzoa	25413	28.____
29.	MPFBJ	zrqao	32541	29.____
30.	JBFPM	oqzra	15432	30.____
31.	BJPMF	qaroz	51234	31.____
32.	PJFMB	rozaq	21435	32.____
33.	FJBMP	zoqra	41532	33.____

48

Questions 34-40.

DIRECTIONS: Questions 34 through 40 are based on the instructions given below. Study the instructions and the sample question; then answer Questions 34 through 40 on the basis of this information

INSTRUCTIONS:

In each of the following Questions 34 through 40, the 3-line name and address in Column 1 is the master-list entry, and the 3-line entry in Column 2 is the information to be checked against the master list.

If there is one line that does not match, mark your answer A.

If there are two lines that do not match, mark your answer B.

If all three lines do not match, mark your answer C.

If the lines all match exactly, mark your answer D.

SAMPLE QUESTION:

Column 1
Mark L. Field
11-09 Prince Park Blvd.
Bronx, N.Y. 11402

Column 2
Mark L. Field
11-99 Prince Park
Bronx, N.Y. 11401

The first lines in each column match exactly. The second lines do not match, since 11-09 does not match 11-99 and Blvd. does not match Way. The third lines do not match either, since 11402 does not match 11401. Therefore, there are two lines that do not match and the correct answer is B.

	Column 1	Column 2	
34.	Jerome A. Jackson 1243 14th Avenue New York, N.Y. 10023	Jerome A. Johnson 1234 14th Avenue New York, N.Y. 10023	34._____
35.	Sophie Strachtheim 33-28 Connecticut Ave. Far Rockaway, N.Y. 11697	Sophie Strachtheim 33-28 Connecticut Ave. Far Rockaway, N.Y. 11697	35._____
36.	Elisabeth N.T. Gorrell 256 Exchange St. New York, N.Y. 10013	Elizabeth N.T. Gorrell 256 Exchange St. New York, N.Y. 10013	36._____
37.	Maria J. Gonzalez 7516 E. Sheepshead Rd. Brooklyn, N.Y. 11240	Maria J. Gonzalez 7516 N. Shepshead Rd. Brooklyn, N.Y. 11240	37._____
38.	Leslie B. Brautenweiler 21 57A Seller Terr. Flushing, N.Y. 11367	Leslie B. Brautenwieler 21-75A Seiler Terr. Flushing, N.J. 11367	38._____

39. Rigoberto J. Peredes
    157 Twin Towers, #18F
    Tottenville, S.I., N.Y.

    Rigoberto J. Peredes
    157 Twin Towers, #18F
    Tottenville, S.I., N.Y.

    39. ___

40. Pietro F. Albino
    P.O. Box 7548
    Floral Park, N.Y. 11005

    Pietro F. Albina
    P.O. Box 7458
    Floral Park, N.Y. 11005

    40. ___

KEY (CORRECT ANSWERS)

1. D	11. A	21. B	31. A
2. C	12. D	22. C	32. D
3. B	13. C	23. C	33. A
4. D	14. B	24. C	34. B
5. B	15. A	25. A	35. D
6. A	16. C	26. B	36. A
7. C	17. C	27. B	37. A
8. D	18. C	28. D	38. C
9. D	19. D	29. C	39. D
10. D	20. C	30. B	40. B

EXAMINATION SECTION
TEST 1

DIRECTIONS: Each question or incomplete statement is followed by several suggested answers or completions. Select the one that BEST answers the question or completes the statement. *PRINT THE LETTER OF THE CORRECT ANSWER IN THE SPACE AT THE RIGHT.*

1. Of the following, the MOST important single factor in any building security program is   1.____

    A. a fool-proof employee identification system
    B. an effective control of entrances and exits
    C. bright illumination of all outside areas
    D. clearly marking public and non-public areas

2. There is general agreement that the BEST criterion of what is a good physical security system in a large public building is   2.____

    A. the number of uniformed officers needed to patrol sensitive areas
    B. how successfully the system prevents rather than detects violations
    C. the number of persons caught in the act of committing criminal offenses
    D. how successfully the system succeeds in maintaining good public relations

3. Which one of the following statements most correctly expresses the CHIEF reason why women were originally made eligible for appointment to the position of officer?   3.____

    A. Certain tasks in security protection can be performed best by assigning women.
    B. More women than men are available to fill many vacancies in this position.
    C. The government wants more women in law enforcement because of their better attendance records.
    D. Women can no longer be barred from any government jobs because of sex.

4. The MOST BASIC purpose of patrol by officers is to   4.____

    A. eliminate as much as possible the opportunity for successful misconduct
    B. investigate criminal complaints and accident cases
    C. give prompt assistance to employees and citizens in distress or requesting their help
    D. take persons into custody who commit criminal offenses against persons and property

5. The highest quality of patrol service is MOST generally obtained by   5.____

    A. frequently changing the post assignments of each officer
    B. assigning officers to posts of equal size
    C. assigning problem officers to the least desirable posts
    D. assigning the same officers to the same posts

6. The one of the following requirements which is MOST essential to the successful performance of patrol duty by individual officers is their   6.____

    A. ability to communicate effectively with higher-level officers
    B. prompt signalling according to a prescribed schedule to insure post coverages at all times

C. knowledge of post conditions and post hazards
D. willingness to cover large areas during periods of critical manpower shortages

7. Officers on patrol are constantly warned to be on the alert for suspicious persons, actions, and circumstances.
With this in mind, a senior officer should emphasize the need for them to

    A. be cautious and suspicious when dealing officially with any civilian regardless of the latter's overt actions or the circumstances surrounding his dealings with the police
    B. keep looking for the unusual persons, actions, and circumstances on their posts and pay less attention to the usual
    C. take aggressive police action immediately against any unusual person or condition detected on their posts, regardless of any other circumstances
    D. become thoroughly familiar with the usual on their posts so as to be better able to detect the unusual

8. Of primary importance in the safeguarding of property from theft is a good central lock and key issuance and control system.
Which one of the following recommendations about maintaining such a control system would be LEAST acceptable?

    A. In selecting locks to be used for the various gates, building, and storage areas, consideration should be given to the amount of security desired.
    B. Master keys should have no markings that will identify them as such and the list of holders of these keys should be frequently reviewed to determine the continuing necessity for the individuals having them.
    C. Whenever keys for outside doors or gates or for other doors which permit access to important buildings and areas are misplaced, the locks should be immediately changed or replaced pending an investigation.
    D. Whenever an employee fails to return a borrowed key at the time specified, a prompt investigation should be made by the security force.

9. In a crowded building, a fire develops in the basement, and smoke enters the crowded rooms on the first floor. Of the following, the BEST action for an officer to take after an alarm is turned in is to

    A. call out a warning that the building is on fire and that everyone should evacuate because of the immediate danger
    B. call all of the officers together for an emergency meeting and discuss a plan of action
    C. immediately call for assistance from the local police station to help in evacuating the crowd
    D. tell everyone that there is a fire in the building next door and that they should move out onto the streets through available exits

10. Which of the following is in a key position to carry out successfully a safety program of an agency? The

    A. building engineer
    B. bureau chiefs
    C. immediate supervisors
    D. public relations director

11. It is GENERALLY considered that a daily roll call inspection, which checks to see that the officers and their equipment are in good order, is

    A. *desirable,* chiefly because it informs the superior officer what men will have to purchase new uniforms within a month
    B. *desirable,* chiefly because the public forms their impressions of the organization from the appearance of the officers
    C. *undesirable,* chiefly because this kind of daily inspection unnecessarily delays officers in getting to their assigned patrol posts
    D. *undesirable,* chiefly because roll call inspection usually misses individuals reporting to work late

12. A supervising officer in giving instructions to a group of officers on the principles of accident investigation remarked, "A conclusion that appears reasonable will often be changed by exploring a factor of apparently little importance".
    Which one of the following precautions does this statement emphasize as MOST important in any accident investigation?

    A. Every accident clue should be fully investigated.
    B. Accidents should not be too promptly investigated.
    C. Only specially trained officers should investigate accidents.
    D. Conclusions about accident causes are highly unreliable.

13. On a rainy day, a senior officer found that 9 of his 50 officers reported to work. What percentage of his officers was ABSENT?

    A. 18%   B. 80%   C. 82%   D. 90%

14. Officer A and Officer B work at the same post on the same days, but their hours are different. Officer A comes to work at 9:00 A.M. and leaves at 5:00 P.M., with a lunch period between 12:15 P.M. and 1:15 P.M. Officer B comes to work at 10:50 A.M. and works until 6:50 P.M., and he takes an hour for lunch between 3:00 P.M. and 4:00 P.M. What is the total amount of time between 9:00 A.M. and 6:50 P.M. that only ONE officer will be on duty?

    A. 4 hours   B. 4 hours and 40 minutes
    C. 5 hours   D. 5 hours and 40 minutes

15. An officer's log recorded the following attendance of 30 officers:

    Monday   20 present;   10 absent
    Tuesday   28 present;   2 absent
    Wednesday   30 present;   0 absent
    Thursday   21 present;   9 absent
    Friday   16 present;   14 absent
    Saturday   11 present;   19 absent
    Sunday   14 present;   16 absent

    On the average, how many men were present on the weekdays (Monday - Friday)?

    A. 21   B. 23   C. 25   D. 27

16. An angry woman is being questioned by an officer when she begins shouting abuses at him.
 The BEST of the following procedures for the officer to follow is to

    A. leave the room until she has cooled off
    B. politely ignore anything she says
    C. place her under arrest by handcuffing her to a fixed object
    D. warn her that he will have to use force to restrain her making remarks

17. Of the following, which is NOT a recommended practice for an officer placing a woman offender under arrest?

    A. Assume that the offender is an innocent and virtuous person and treat her accordingly.
    B. Protect himself from attack by the woman.
    C. Refrain from using excessive physical force on the offender.
    D. Make the public aware that he is not abusing the woman.

Questions 18-21.

DIRECTIONS: Questions 18 through 21 are to be answered SOLELY on the basis of the following passage.

Specific measures for prevention of pilferage will be based on careful analysis of the conditions at each agency. The most practical and effective method to control casual pilferage is the establishment of psychological deterrents.

One of the most common means of discouraging casual pilferage is to search individuals leaving the agency at unannounced times and places. These spot searches may occasionally detect attempts at theft but greater value is realized by bringing to the attention of individuals the fact that they may be apprehended if they do attempt the illegal removal of property.

An aggressive security education program is an effective means of convincing employees that they have much more to lose than they do to gain by engaging in acts of theft. It is important for all employees to realize that pilferage is morally wrong no matter how insignificant the value of the item which is taken. In establishing any deterrent to casual pilferage, security officers must not lose sight of the fact that most employees are honest and disapprove of thievery. Mutual respect between security personnel and other employees of the agency must be maintained if the facility is to be protected from other more dangerous forms of human hazards. Any security measure which infringes on the human rights or dignity of others will jeopardize, rather than enhance, the overall protection of the agency.

18. The $100,000 yearly inventory of an agency revealed that $50 worth of goods had been stolen; the only individuals with access to the stolen materials were the employees. Of the following measures, which would the author of the preceding paragraph MOST likely recommend to a security officer?

    A. Conduct an intensive investigation of all employees to find the culprit.
    B. Make a record of the theft, but take no investigative or disciplinary action against any employee.
    C. Place a tight security check on all future movements of personnel.
    D. Remove the remainder of the material to an area with much greater security.

19. What does the passage imply is the percentage of employees whom a security officer should expect to be honest?

    A. No employee can be expected to be honest all of the time
    B. Just 50%
    C. Less than 50%
    D. More than 50%

19._____

20. According to the passage, the security officer would use which of the following methods to minimize theft in buildings with many exits when his staff is very small?

    A. Conduct an inventory of all material and place a guard near that which is most likely to be pilfered.
    B. Inform employees of the consequences of legal prosecution for pilfering.
    C. Close off the unimportant exits and have all his men concentrate on a few exits.
    D. Place a guard at each exit and conduct a casual search of individuals leaving the premises.

20._____

21. Of the following, the title BEST suited for this passage is:

    A. Control Measures for Casual Pilfering
    B. Detecting the Potential Pilferer
    C. Financial losses Resulting from Pilfering
    D. The Use of Moral Persuasion in Physical Security

21._____

22. Of the following first aid procedures, which will cause the GREATEST harm in treating a fracture?

    A. Control hemorrhages by applying direct pressure
    B. Keep the broken portion from moving about
    C. Reset a protruding bone by pressing it back into place
    D. Treat the suffering person for shock

22._____

23. During a snowstorm, a man comes to you complaining of frostbitten hands. PROPER first aid treatment in this case is to

    A. place the hands under hot running water
    B. place the hands in lukewarm water
    C. call a hospital and wait for medical aid
    D. rub the hands in melting snow

23._____

24. While on duty, an officer sees a woman apparently in a state of shock. Of the following, which one is NOT a symptom of shock?

    A. Eyes lacking luster
    B. A cold, moist forehead
    C. A shallow, irregular breathing
    D. A strong, throbbing pulse

24._____

25. You notice a man entering your building who begins coughing violently, has shortness of breath, and complains of severe chest pains.
    These symptoms are GENERALLY indicative of

    A. a heart attack   B. a stroke
    C. internal bleeding   D. an epileptic seizure

25._____

26. When an officer is required to record the rolled fingerprint impressions of a prisoner on the standard fingerprint form, the technique recommended by the F.B.I, as MOST likely to result in obtaining clear impressions is to roll

   A. all fingers away from the center of the prisoner's body
   B. all fingers toward the center of the prisoner's body
   C. the thumbs away from and the other fingers toward the center of the prisoner's body
   D. the thumbs toward and the other fingers away from the center of the prisoner's body

27. The principle which underlies the operation and use of a lie detector machine is that

   A. a person who is not telling the truth will be able to give a consistent story
   B. a guilty mind will unconsciously associate ideas in a very indicative manner
   C. the presence of emotional stress in a person will result in certain abnormal physical reactions
   D. many individuals are not afraid to lie

Questions 28-32.

DIRECTIONS: Questions 28 through 32 are based SOLELY on the following diagram and the paragraph preceding this group of questions. The paragraph will be divided into two statements. Statement one (1) consists of information given to the senior officer by an agency director; *this information will detail the specific security objectives the senior officer has to meet.* Statement two (2) gives the resources available to the senior officer.

NOTE: The questions are correctly answered only when all of the agency's objectives have been met and when the officer has used all his resources efficiently (i.e., to their maximum effectiveness) in meeting these objectives. All X's in the diagram indicate possible locations of officers' posts. Each X has a corresponding number which is to be used when referring to that location.

DIAGRAM

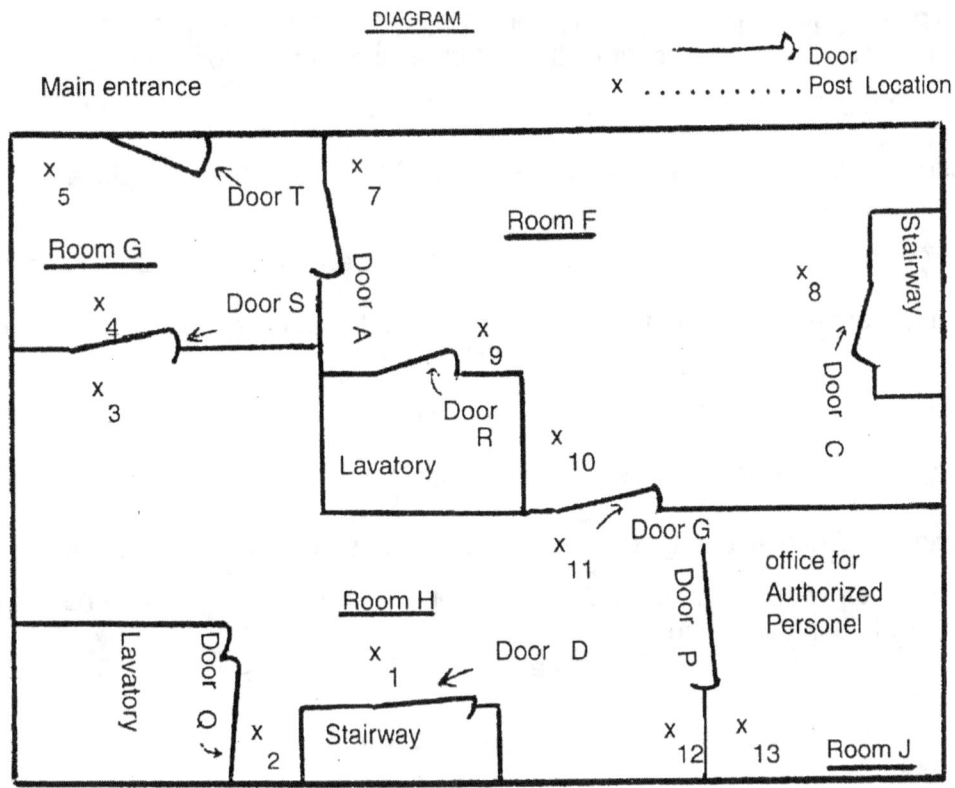

PARAGRAPH

PARAGRAPH

STATEMENT 1: Room G will be the public intake room from which persons will be directed to Room F or Room H; under no circumstances are they to enter the wrong room, and they are not to move from Room F to Room H or vice-versa. A minimum of two officers must be in each room frequented by the public at all times, and they are to keep unauthorized individuals from going to the second floor or into restricted areas. All usable entrances or exits must be covered.

STATEMENT 2: The senior officer can lock any door except the main entrance and stairway doors. He has a staff of five officers to carry out these operations.

NOTE: The senior officer is available for guard duty. Room J is an active office.

28. According to the instructions, how many officers should be assigned inside the office for authorized personnel (Room J)?

    A. 0   B. 1   C. 2   D. 3

28._____

29. In order to keep the public from moving between Room F and Room H, which door(s) can be locked without interfering with normal office operations? Door

    A. G   B. P   C. R and Q   D. S

29._____

30. When placing officers in Room H, the only way the senior officer can satisfy the agency's objectives and his manpower limitations is by placing men at locations

    A. 1 and 3　　B. 1 and 12　　C. 3 and 11　　D. 11 and 12

31. In accordance with the instructions, the LEAST effective locations to place officers in Room F are locations

    A. 7 and 9　　B. 7 and 10　　C. 8 and 9　　D. 9 and 10

32. In which room is it MOST difficult for each of the officers to see all the movements of the public? Room

    A. G　　B. F　　C. H　　D. J

33. According to its own provisions, the Penal Law of the State has a number of general purposes.
    It would be LEAST accurate to state that one of these general purposes is to

    A. give fair warning of the nature of the conduct forbidden and the penalties authorized upon conviction
    B. define the act or omission and accompanying mental state which constitute each offense
    C. regulate the procedure which governs the arrest, trial and punishment of convicted offenders
    D. insure the public safety by preventing the commission of offenses through the deterrent influence of the sentences authorized upon conviction

34. Officers must be well-informed about the meaning of certain terms in connection with their enforcement duties. Which one of the following statements about such terms would be MOST accurate according to the Penal Law of the State? A(n)

    A. offense is always a crime
    B. offense is always a violation
    C. violation is never a crime
    D. felony is never an offense

35. According to the Penal Law of the State, the one of the following elements which must ALWAYS be present in order to justify the arrest of a person for criminal assault is

    A. the infliction of an actual physical injury
    B. an intent to cause an injury
    C. a threat to inflict a physical injury
    D. the use of some kind of weapon

36. A recent law of the State defines who are police officers and who are peace officers. The official title of this law is: The

    A. Criminal Code of Procedure
    B. Law of Criminal Procedure
    C. Criminal Procedure Law
    D. Code of Criminal Procedure

37. If you are required to appear in court to testify as the complainant in a criminal action, it would be MOST important for you to

    A. confine your answers to the questions asked when you are testifying
    B. help the prosecutor even if some exaggeration in your testimony may be necessary
    C. be as fair as possible to the defendant even if some details have to be omitted from your testimony
    D. avoid contradicting other witnesses testifying against the defendant

38. A senior officer is asked by the television news media to explain to the public what happened on his post during an important incident.
    When speaking with departmental permission in front of the tape recorders and cameras, the senior officer can give the MOST favorable impression of himself and his department by

    A. refusing to answer any questions but remaining calm in front of the cameras
    B. giving a detailed report of the wrong decisions made by his agency for handling the particular incident
    C. presenting the appropriate factual information in a competent way
    D. telling what should have been done during the incident and how such incidents will be handled in the future

39. Of the following suggested guidelines for officers, the one which is LEAST likely to be effective in promoting good manners and courtesy in their daily contacts with the public is:

    A. Treat inquiries by telephone in the same manner as those made in person
    B. Never look into the face of the person to whom you are speaking
    C. Never give misinformation in answer to any inquiry on a matter on which you are uncertain of the facts
    D. Show respect and consideration in both trivial and important contacts with the public

40. Assume you are an officer who has had a record of submitting late weekly reports and that you are given an order by your supervisor which is addressed to all line officers. The order states that weekly reports will be replaced by twice-weekly reports.
    The MOST logical conclusion for you to make, of the following, is:

    A. Fully detailed information was missing from your past reports
    B. Most officers have submitted late reports
    C. The supervisor needs more timely information
    D. The supervisor is attempting to punish you for your past late reports

41. A young man with long hair and "mod" clothing makes a complaint to an officer about the rudeness of another officer.
    If the senior officer is not on the premises, the officer receiving the complaint should

    A. consult with the officer who is being accused to see if the youth's story is true
    B. refer the young man to central headquarters
    C. record the complaint made against his fellow officer and ask the youth to wait until he can locate the senior officer
    D. search for the senior officer and bring him back to the site of the complainant

42. During a demonstration, which area should ALWAYS be kept clear of demonstrators?

   A. Water fountains
   B. Seating areas
   C. Doorways
   D. Restrooms

43. During demonstrations, an officer's MOST important duty is to

   A. aid the agency's employees to perform their duties
   B. promptly arrest those who might cause incidents
   C. promptly disperse the crowds of demonstrators
   D. keep the demonstrators from disrupting order

44. Of the following, what is the FIRST action a senior officer should take if a demonstration develops in his area without advance warning?

   A. Call for additional assistance from the police department
   B. Find the leaders of the demonstrators and discuss their demands
   C. See if the demonstrators intend to break the law
   D. Inform his superiors of the event taking place

45. If a senior officer is informed in the morning that a demonstration will take place during the afternoon at his assigned location, he should assemble his officers to discuss the nature and aspects of this demonstration. Of the following, the subject which it is LEAST important to discuss during this meeting is

   A. making a good impression if an officer is called before the television cameras for a personal interview
   B. the known facts and causes of the demonstration
   C. the attitude and expected behavior of the demonstrators
   D. the individual responsibilities of the officers during the demonstration

46. A male officer has probable reason to believe that a group of women occupying the ladies' toilet are using illicit drugs.
The BEST action, of the following, for the officer to take is to

   A. call for assistance and, with the aid of such assistance, enter the toilet and escort the occupants outside
   B. ignore the situation but recommend that the ladies' toilet be closed temporarily
   C. immediately rush into the ladies' toilet and search the occupants therein
   D. knock on the door of the ladies' toilet and ask their permission to enter so that he will not be accused of trying to molest them

47. Assume that you know that a group of demonstrators will not cooperate with your request to throw handbills in a waste basket instead of on the sidewalk. You ask one of the leaders of the group, who agrees with you, to speak to the demonstrators and ask for their cooperation in this matter.
Your request of the group leader is

   A. *desirable,* chiefly because an officer needs civilians to control the public since the officer is usually unfriendly to the views of public groups
   B. *undesirable,* chiefly because an officer should never request a civilian to perform his duties
   C. *desirable,* chiefly because the appeal of an acknowledged leader helps in gaining group cooperation

D. *undesirable,* chiefly because an institutional leader is motivated to maneuver a situation to gain his own personal advantage

48. A vague letter received from a female employee in the agency accuses an officer of improper conduct.
The initial investigative interview by the senior officer assigned to check the accusation should GENERALLY be with the

   A. accused officer
   B. female employee
   C. highest superior about disciplinary action against the officer
   D. immediate supervisor of the female employee

Questions 49-50.

DIRECTIONS: Questions 49 and 50 are to be answered SOLELY on the basis of the information in the following paragraph.

The personal conduct of each member of the Department is the primary factor in promoting desirable police-community relations. Tact, patience, and courtesy shall be strictly observed under all circumstances. A favorable public attitude toward the police must be earned; it is influenced by the personal conduct and attitude of each member of the force, by his personal integrity and courteous manner, by his respect for due process of law, by his devotion to the principles of justice, fairness, and impartiality.

49. According to the preceding paragraph, what is the BEST action an officer can take in dealing with people in a neighborhood?

   A. Assist neighborhood residents by doing favors for them.
   B. Give special attention to the community leaders in order to be able to control them effectively.
   C. Behave in an appropriate manner and give all community members the same just treatment.
   D. Prepare a plan detailing what he, the officer, wants to do for the community and submit it for approval.

50. As used in the paragraph, the word *impartiality* means *most nearly*

   A. observant   B. unbiased
   C. righteousness   D. honesty

KEY (CORRECT ANSWERS)

1. B	11. B	21. A	31. D	41. C
2. B	12. A	22. C	32. C	42. C
3. A	13. C	23. B	33. C	43. D
4. A	14. D	24. D	34. C	44. D
5. D	15. B	25. A	35. A	45. A
6. C	16. B	26. D	36. C	46. A
7. D	17. A	27. C	37. A	47. C
8. C	18. B	28. A	38. C	48. B
9. D	19. D	29. A	39. B	49. C
10. C	20. B	30. B	40. C	50. B

TEST 2

DIRECTIONS: Each question or incomplete statement is followed by several suggested answers or completions. Select the one that BEST answers the question or completes the statement. *PRINT THE LETTER OF THE CORRECT ANSWER IN THE SPACE AT THE RIGHT.*

Questions 1-5.

DIRECTIONS: Questions 1 through 5 consist of short paragraphs. Each paragraph contains one word which is INCORRECTLY used because it is NOT in keeping with the meaning of the paragraph. Find the word in each paragraph which is INCORRECTLY used, and then select as the answer the suggested word which should be substituted for the incorrectly used word.

SAMPLE QUESTION

In determining who is to do the work in your unit, you will have to decide just who does what from day to day. One of your lowest responsibilities is to assign work so that everybody gets a fair share and that everyone can do his part well.
    A. new   B. old   C. important   D. performance

EXPLANATION

The word which is NOT in keeping with the meaning of the paragraph is "lowest". This is the INCORRECTLY used word. The suggested word "important" would be in keeping with the meaning of the paragraph and should be substituted for "lowest". Therefore, the CORRECT answer is Choice C.

1. If really good practice in the elimination of preventable injuries is to be achieved and held in any establishment, top management must refuse full and definite responsibility and must apply a good share of its attention to the task.

    A. accept   B. avoidable   C. duties   D. problem

1._____

2. Recording the human face for identification is by no means the only service performed by the camera in the field of investigation. When the trial of any issue takes place, a word picture is sought to be distorted to the court of incidents, occurrences, or events which are in dispute.

    A. appeals   B. description
    C. portrayed   D. deranged

2._____

3. In the collection of physical evidence, it cannot be emphasized too strongly that a haphazard systematic search at the scene of the crime is vital. Nothing must be overlooked. Often the only leads in a case will come from the results of this search.

    A. important   B. investigation
    C. proof   D. thorough

3._____

4. If an investigator has reason to suspect that the witness is mentally stable or a habitual drunkard, he should leave no stone unturned in his investigation to determine if the witness was under the influence of liquor or drugs, or was mentally unbalanced either at the time of the occurrence to which he testified or at the time of the trial.

    A. accused   B. clue   C. deranged   D. question

4._____

5. The use of records is a valuable step in crime investigation and is the main reason every department should maintain accurate reports. Crimes are not committed through the use of departmental records alone but from the use of all records, of almost every type, wherever they may be found and whenever they give any incidental information regarding the criminal.

    A. accidental   B. necessary   C. reported   D. solved

Questions 6-8.

DIRECTIONS: Questions 6 through 8 are to be answered SOLELY on the basis of the following passage.

    The mass media are an integral part of the daily life of virtually every American. Among these media, the youngest, television, is the most persuasive. Ninety-five percent of American homes have at least one television set, and on the average that set is in use for about 40 hours each week. The central place of television in American life makes this medium the focal point of a growing national concern over the effects of media portrayals of violence on the values, attitudes, and behavior of an ever increasing audience.

    In our concern about violence and its causes, it is easy to make television a scapegoat. But we emphasise the fact that there is no simple answer to the problem of violence -- no single explanation of its causes, and no single prescription for its control. It should be remembered that America also experienced high levels of crime and violence in periods before the advent of television.

    The problem of balance, taste, and artistic merit in entertaining programs on television are complex. We cannot <u>countenance</u> government censorship of television. Nor would we seek to impose arbitrary limitations on programming which might jeopardize television's ability to deal in dramatic presentations with controversial social issues. Nonetheless, we are deeply troubled by television's constant portrayal of violence, not in any genuine attempt to focus artistic expression on the human condition, but rather in pandering to a public preoccupation with violence that television itself has helped to generate.

6. According to the passage, television uses violence MAINLY

    A. to highlight the reality of everyday existence
    B. to satisfy the audience's hunger for destructive action
    C. to shape the values and attitudes of the public
    D. when it films documentaries concerning human conflict

7. Which one of the following statements is BEST supported by this passage?

    A. Early American history reveals a crime pattern which is not related to television.
    B. Programs should give presentations of social issues and never portray violent acts.
    C. Television has proven that entertainment programs can easily make the balance between taste and artistic merit a simple matter.
    D. Values and behavior should be regulated by governmental censorship.

8. Of the following, which word has the same meaning as <u>countenance</u> as it is used in the above passage?

    A. approve   B. exhibit   C. oppose   D. reject

Questions 9-12.

DIRECTIONS: Questions 9 through 12 are to be answered SOLELY on the basis of the following graph relating to the burglary rate in the city, 2003 to 2008, inclusive.

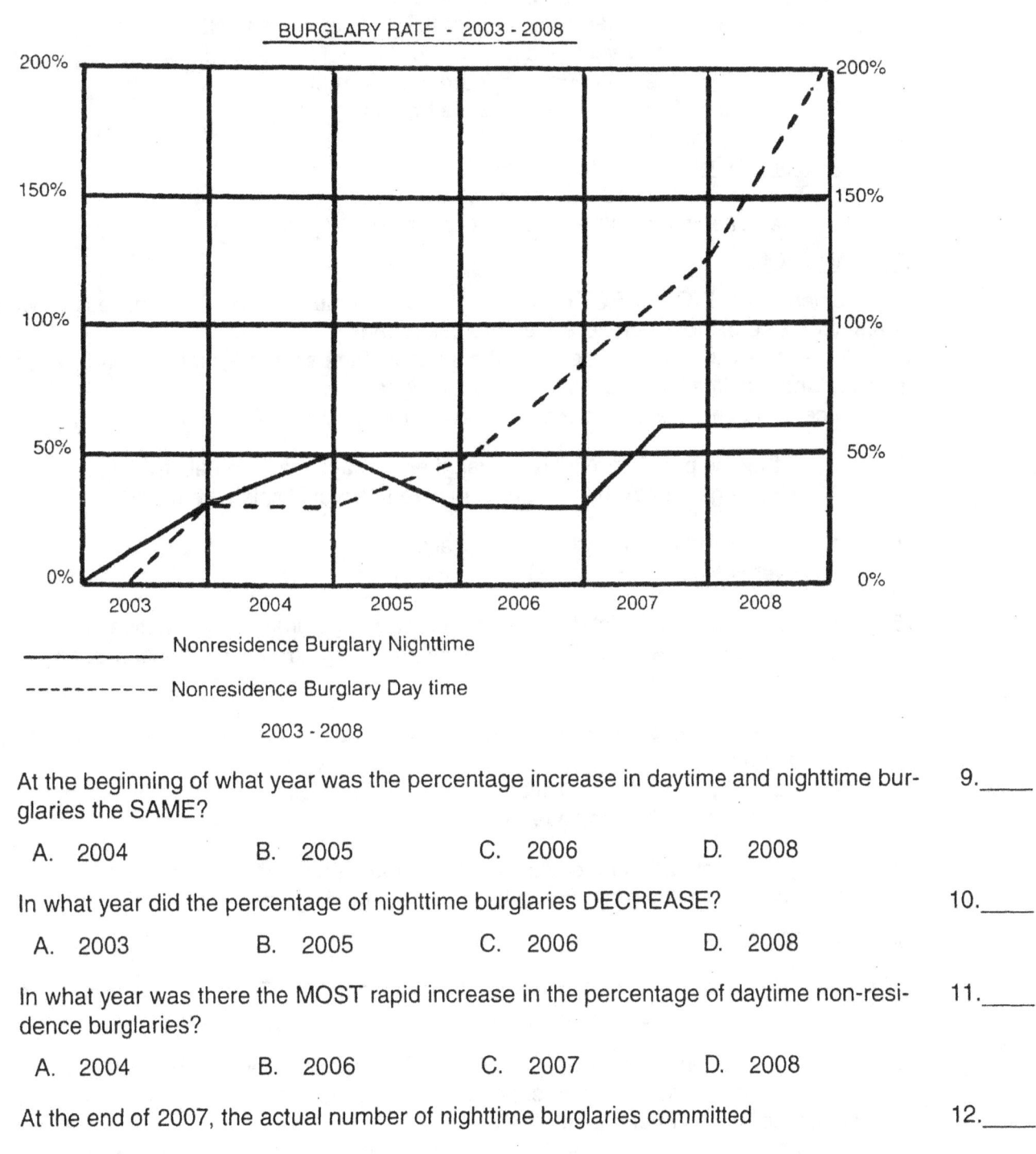

2003 - 2008

9. At the beginning of what year was the percentage increase in daytime and nighttime burglaries the SAME?

    A. 2004   B. 2005   C. 2006   D. 2008

10. In what year did the percentage of nighttime burglaries DECREASE?

    A. 2003   B. 2005   C. 2006   D. 2008

11. In what year was there the MOST rapid increase in the percentage of daytime non-residence burglaries?

    A. 2004   B. 2006   C. 2007   D. 2008

12. At the end of 2007, the actual number of nighttime burglaries committed

    A. was about 20%
    B. was 40%
    C. was 400
    D. cannot be determined from the information given

Questions 13-17.

DIRECTIONS: Questions 13 through 17 consist of two sentences numbered 1 and 2 taken from police officers' reports. Some of these sentences are correct according to ordinary formal English usage. Other sentences are incorrect because they contain errors in English usage or punctuation. Consider a sentence correct if it contains no errors in English usage or punctuation even if there may be other ways of writing the sentence correctly. Mark your answer to each question in the space at the right as follows:
- A. If only sentence 1 is correct, but not sentence 2
- B. If only sentence 2 is correct, but not sentence 1
- C. If sentences 1 and 2 are both correct
- D. If sentences 1 and 2 are both incorrect

SAMPLE QUESTION
1. The woman claimed that the purse was her's.
2. Everyone of the new officers was assigned to a patrol post.

EXPLANATION

Sentence 1 is INCORRECT because of an error in punctuation. The possessive words, "ours, yours, hers, theirs," do not have the apostrophe (').

Sentence 2 is CORRECT because the subject of the sentence is "Everyone" which is singular and requires the singular verb "was assigned".

Since only sentence 2 is correct, but not sentence 1, the CORRECT answer is B.

13.
1. Either the patrolman or his sergeant are always ready to help the public.
2. The sergeant asked the patrolman when he would finish the report.

14.
1. The injured man could not hardly talk.
2. Every officer had ought to hand in their reports on time.

15.
1. Approaching the victim of the assault, two large bruises were noticed by me.
2. The prisoner was arrested for assault, resisting arrest, and use of a deadly weapon.

16.
1. A copy of the orders, which had been prepared by the captain, was given to each patrolman.
2. It's always necessary to inform an arrested person of his constitutional rights before asking him any questions.

17.
1. To prevent further bleeding, I applied a tourniquet tothe wound.
2. John Rano a senior officer was on duty at the time of the accident.

Questions 18-25.

DIRECTIONS: Answer each of Questions 18 through 25 SOLELY on the basis of the statement preceding the questions.

18. The criminal is one whose habits have been erroneously developed or, we should say, developed in anti-social patterns, and therefore the task of dealing with him is not one of punishment, but of treatment.
The basic principle expressed in this statement is BEST illustrated by the

- A. emphasis upon rehabilitation in penal institutions
- B. prevalence of capital punishment for murder
- C. practice of imposing heavy fines for minor violations
- D. legal provision for trial by jury in criminal cases

19. The writ of habeas corpus is one of the great guarantees of personal liberty. Of the following, the BEST justification for this statement is that the writ of habeas corpus is frequently used to

    A. compel the appearance in court of witnesses who are outside the state
    B. obtain the production of books and records at a criminal trial
    C. secure the release of a person improperly held in custody
    D. prevent the use of deception in obtaining testimony of reluctant witnesses

20. Fifteen persons suffered effects of carbon dioxide asphyxiation shortly before noon recently in a seventh-floor pressing shop. The accident occurred in a closed room where six steam presses were in operation. Four men and one woman were overcome.
    Of the following, the MOST probable reason for the fact that so many people were affected simultaneously is that

    A. women evidently show more resistance to the effects of carbon dioxide than men
    B. carbon dioxide is an odorless and colorless gas
    C. carbon dioxide is lighter than air
    D. carbon dioxide works more quickly at higher altitudes

21. Lay the patient on his stomach, one arm extended directly overhead, the other arm bent at the elbow, and with the face turned outward and resting on hand or forearm.
    To the officer who is skilled at administering first aid, these instructions should IMMEDIATELY suggest

    A. application of artificial respiration
    B. treatment for third degree burns of the arm
    C. setting a dislocated shoulder
    D. control of capillary bleeding in the stomach

22. The soda and acid fire extinguisher is the hand extinguisher most commonly used by officers. The main body of the cylinder is filled with a mixture of water and bicarbonate of soda. In a separate interior compartment, at the top, is a small bottle of sulphuric acid. When the extinguisher is inverted, the acid spills into the solution below and starts a chemical reaction. The carbon dioxide thereby generated forces the solution from the extinguisher.
    The officer who understands the operation of this fire extinguisher should know that it is LEAST likely to operate properly

    A. in basements or cellars
    B. in extremely cold weather
    C. when the reaction is of a chemical nature
    D. when the bicarbonate of soda is in solution

23. Suppose that, at a training lecture, you are told that many of the men in our penal institutions today are second and third offenders.
    Of the following, the MOST valid inference you can make SOLELY on the basis of this statement is that

    A. second offenders are not easily apprehended
    B. patterns of human behavior are not easily changed
    C. modern laws are not sufficiently flexible
    D. laws do not breed crimes

24. In all societies of our level of culture, acts are committed which arouse censure severe enough to take the form of punishment by the government. Such acts are crimes, not because of their inherent nature, but because of their ability to arouse resentment and to stimulate repressive measures.
Of the following, the MOST valid inference which can be drawn from this statement is that

   A. society unjustly punishes acts which are inherently criminal
   B. many acts are not crimes but are punished by society because such acts threaten the lives of innocent people
   C. only modern society has a level of culture
   D. societies sometimes disagree as to what acts are crimes

25. Crime cannot be measured directly. Its amount must be inferred from the frequency of some occurrence connected with it; for example, crimes brought to the attention of the police, persons arrested, prosecutions, convictions, and other dispositions, such as probation or commitment. Each of these may be used as an index of the amount of crime.
SOLELY on the basis of the foregoing statement, it is MOST correct to state that

   A. the incidence of crime cannot be estimated with any accuracy
   B. the number of commitments is usually greater than the number of probationary sentences
   C. the amount of crime is ordinarily directly correlated with the number of persons arrested
   D. a joint consideration of crimes brought to the attention of the police and the number of prosecutions undertaken gives little indication of the amount of crime in a locality

KEY (CORRECT ANSWERS)

1. B
2. A
3. D
4. C
5. D

6. B
7. A
8. A
9. A
10. B

11. D
12. D
13. D
14. D
15. B

16. C
17. A
18. A
19. C
20. B

21. A
22. B
23. B
24. D
25. C

EXAMINATION SECTION
TEST 1

DIRECTIONS: Each question or incomplete statement is followed by several suggested answers or completions. Select the one that BEST answers the question or completes the statement. *PRINT THE LETTER OF THE CORRECT ANSWER IN THE SPACE AT THE RIGHT.*

1. The officer who investigates accidents is always required to make a complete and accurate report.
   Of the following, the BEST reason for this procedure is to

   A. protect the operating agency against possible false claims
   B. provide a file of incidents which can be used as basic material for an accident prevention campaign
   C. provide the management with concrete evidence of violations of the rules by employees
   D. indicate what repairs need to be made

2. It is suggested that an officer keep all persons away from the area of an accident until an investigation has been completed.
   This suggested procedure is

   A. *good;* witnesses will be more likely to agree on a single story
   B. *bad;* such action blocks traffic flow and causes congestion
   C. *good;* objects of possible use as evidence will be protected from damage or loss
   D. *bad;* the flow of normal pedestrian traffic provides an opportunity for an investigator to determine the cause of the accident

3. A man having business with your agency is arguing with you and accuses you of being prejudiced against him. Although you explain to him that this is not so, he demands to see your supervisor.
   Of the following, the BEST course of action for you to take is to

   A. continue arguing with him until you have worn him out or convinced him
   B. take him to your supervisor
   C. ignore him and walk away from him to another part of the office
   D. escort him out of the office

4. An officer receives instructions from his supervisor which he does not fully understand.
   For the officer to ask for a further explanation would be

   A. *good;* chiefly because his supervisor will be impressed with his interest in his work
   B. *poor;* chiefly because the time of the supervisor will be needlessly wasted
   C. *good;* chiefly because proper performance depends on full understanding of the work to be done
   D. *poor;* chiefly because officers should be able to think for themselves

5. A person is making a complaint to an officer which seems unreasonable and of little importance.
   Of the following, the BEST action for the officer to take is to

A. criticize the person making the complaint for taking up his valuable time
B. laugh over the matter to show that the complaint is minor and silly
C. tell the person that anyone responsible for his grievance will be prosecuted
D. listen to the person making the complaint and tell him that the matter will be investigated

6. A member of the department shall not indulge in intoxicating liquor while in uniform. A member of the department is not required to wear a uniform, and a uniformed member while out of uniform shall not indulge in intoxicants to an extent unfitting him for duty.
Of the following, the MOST correct interpretation of this rule is that a

   A. member, off duty, not in uniform, may drink intoxicating liquor
   B. member, not on duty, but in uniform, may drink intoxicating liquor
   C. member, on duty, in uniform, may drink intoxicants
   D. uniformed member, in civilian clothes, may not drink intoxicants

7. You have a suggestion for an important change which you believe will improve a certain procedure in your agency. Of the following, the next course of action for you to take is to

   A. try it out yourself
   B. submit the suggestion to your immediate supervisor
   C. write a letter to the head of your agency asking for his approval
   D. wait until you are asked for suggestions before submitting this one

8. An officer shall study maps and literature concerning his assigned area and the streets and points of interest nearby.
Of the following, the BEST reason for this rule is that

   A. the officer will be better able to give correct information to persons desiring it
   B. the officer will be better able to drive a vehicle in the area
   C. the officer will not lose interest in his work
   D. supervisors will not need to train the officers in this subject

9. In asking a witness to a crime to identify a suspect, it is a common practice to place the suspect with a group of persons and ask the witness to pick out the person in question.
Of the following, the BEST reason for this practice is that it will

   A. make the identification more reliable than if the witness were shown the suspect alone
   B. protect the witness against reprisals
   C. make sure that the witness is telling the truth
   D. help select other participants in the crime at the same time

10. It is most important for all officers to obey the "Rules and Regulations" of their agency.
Of the following, the BEST reason for this statement is that

    A. supervisors will not need to train their new officers
    B. officers will never have to use their own judgment
    C. uniform procedures will be followed
    D. officers will not need to ask their supervisors for assistance

Questions 11-13.

DIRECTIONS: Answer questions 11 to 13 SOLELY on the basis of the following paragraph.

All members of the police force must recognize that the people, through their representatives, hire and pay the police and that, as in any other employment, there must exist a proper employer-employee relationship. The police officer must understand that the essence of a correct police attitude is a willingness to serve, but at the same time, he should distinguish between service and servility, and between courtesy and softness. He must be firm but also courteous, avoiding even an appearance of rudeness. He should develop a position that is friendly and unbiased, pleasant and sympathetic, in his relations with the general public, but firm and impersonal on occasions calling for regulation and control. A police officer should understand that his primary purpose is to prevent violations, not to arrest people. He should recognize the line of demarcation between a police function and passing judgment which is a court function. On the other side, a public that cooperates with the police, that supports them in their efforts and that observes laws and regulations, may be said to have a desirable attitude.

11. In accordance with this paragraph, the PROPER attitude for a police officer to take is to   11._____
    A. be pleasant and sympathetic at all times
    B. be friendly, firm, and impartial
    C. be stern and severe in meting out justice to all
    D. avoid being rude, except in those cases where the public is uncooperative

12. Assume that an officer is assigned by his superior officer to a busy traffic intersection and   12._____
    is warned to be on the lookout for motorists who skip the light or who are speeding.
    According to this paragraph, it would be proper for the officer in this assignment to
    A. give a summons to every motorist whose ear was crossing when the light changed
    B. hide behind a truck and wait for drivers who violate traffic laws
    C. select at random motorists who seem to be impatient and lecture them sternly on traffic safety
    D. stand on post in order to deter violations and give offenders a summons or a warning as required

13. According to this paragraph, a police officer must realize that the primary purpose of   13._____
    police work is to
    A. provide proper police service in a courteous manner
    B. decide whether those who violate the law should be punished
    C. arrest those who violate laws
    D. establish a proper employer-employee relationship

Questions 14-15.

DIRECTIONS: Answer questions 14 and 15 SOLELY on the basis of the following paragraph.

If a motor vehicle fails to pass inspection, the owner will be given a rejection notice by the inspection station. Repairs must be made within ten days after this notice is issued. It is not necessary to have the required adjustment or repairs made at the station where the inspection occurred. The vehicle may be taken to any other garage. Re-inspection after repairs may be made at any official inspection station, not necessarily the same station which made the initial inspection. The registration of any motor vehicle for which an inspection sticker has not been obtained as required, or which is not repaired and inspected within ten days after inspection indicates defects, is subject to suspension. A vehicle cannot be used on public highways while its registration is under suspension.

14. According to the above paragraph, the owner of a car which does NOT pass inspection must

    A. have repairs made at the same station which rejected his car
    B. take the car to another station and have it re-inspected
    C. have repairs made anywhere and then have the car re-inspected
    D. not use the car on a public highway until the necessary repairs have been made

15. According to the above paragraph, the one of the following which may be cause for suspension of the registration of a vehicle is that

    A. an inspection sticker was issued before the rejection notice had been in force for ten days
    B. it was not re-inspected by the station that rejected it originally
    C. it was not re-inspected either by the station that rejected it originally or by the garage which made the repairs
    D. it has not had defective parts repaired within ten days after inspection

Questions 16-20.

DIRECTIONS: Answer questions 16 to 20 SOLELY on the basis of the following paragraph.

If we are to study crime in its widest social setting, we will find a variety of conduct which, although criminal in the legal sense, is not offensive to the moral conscience of a considerable number of persons. Traffic violations, for example, do not brand the offender as guilty of moral offense. In fact, the recipient of a traffic ticket is usually simply the subject of some good-natured joking by his friends. Although there may be indignation among certain groups of citizens against gambling and liquor law violations, these activities are often tolerated, if not openly supported, by the more numerous residents of the community. Indeed, certain social and service clubs regularly conduct gambling games and lotteries for the purpose of raising funds. Some communities regard violations involving the sale of liquor with little concern in order to profit from increased license fees and taxes paid by dealers. The thousand and one forms of political graft and corruption which infest our urban centers only occasionally arouse public condemnation and official action.

16. According to the paragraph, all types of illegal conduct are

    A. condemned by all elements of the community
    B. considered a moral offense, although some are tolerated by a few citizens
    C. violations of the law, but some are acceptable to certain elements of the community
    D. found in a social setting which is not punishable by law

17. According to the paragraph, traffic violations are generally considered by society as

    A. crimes requiring the maximum penalty set by the law
    B. more serious than violations of the liquor laws

C. offenses against the morals of the community
D. relatively minor offenses requiring minimum punishment

18. According to the paragraph, a lottery conducted for the purpose of raising funds for a church

    A. is considered a serious violation of law
    B. may be tolerated by a community which has laws against gambling
    C. may be conducted under special laws demanded by the more numerous residents of a community
    D. arouses indignation in most communities

19. On the basis of the paragraph, the MOST likely reaction in the community to a police raid on a gambling casino would be

    A. more an attitude of indifference than interest in the raid
    B. general approval of the raid
    C. condemnation of the raid by most people
    D. demand for further action since this raid is not sufficient to end gambling activities

20. The one of the following which BEST describes the central thought of this paragraph and would be MOST suitable as a title for it is

    A. CRIME AND THE POLICE
    B. PUBLIC CONDEMNATION OF GRAFT AND CORRUPTION
    C. GAMBLING IS NOT ALWAYS A VICIOUS BUSINESS
    D. PUBLIC ATTITUDE TOWARD LAW VIOLATIONS

18.____

19.____

20.____

Questions 21-23.

DIRECTIONS: Answer questions 21 to 23 SOLELY on the basis of the following paragraph.

The law enforcement agency is one of the most important agencies in the field of juvenile delinquency prevention. This is so not because of the social work connected with this problem, however, for this is not a police matter, but because the officers are usually the first to come in contact with the delinquent. The manner of arrest and detention makes a deep impression upon him and affects his life-long attitude toward society and the law. The juvenile court is perhaps the most important agency in this work. Contrary to the general opinion, however, it is not primarily concerned with putting children into correctional schools. The main purpose of the juvenile court is to save the child and to develop his emotional make-up in order that he can grow up to be a decent and well-balanced citizen. The system of probation is the means whereby the court seeks to accomplish these goals.

21. According to this paragraph, police work is an important part of a program to prevent juvenile delinquency because

    A. social work is no longer considered important in juvenile delinquency prevention
    B. police officers are the first to have contact with the delinquent
    C. police officers jail the offender in order to be able to change his attitude toward society and the law
    D. it is the first step in placing the delinquent in jail

21.____

22. According to this paragraph, the CHIEF purpose of the juvenile court is to

　　A. punish the child for his offense
　　B. select a suitable correctional school for the delinquent
　　C. use available means to help the delinquent become a better person
　　D. provide psychiatric care for the delinquent

23. According to this paragraph, the juvenile court directs the development of delinquents under its care CHIEFLY by

　　A. placing the child under probation
　　B. sending the child to a correctional school
　　C. keeping the delinquent in prison
　　D. returning the child to his home

Questions 24-27.

DIRECTIONS: Answer questions 24 to 27 SOLELY on the basis of the following paragraph.

When a vehicle has been disabled in the tunnel, the officer on patrol in this zone shall press the EMERGENCY TRUCK light button. In the fast lane, red lights will go on throughout the tunnel; in the slow lane, amber lights will go on throughout the tunnel. The yellow zone light will go on at each signal control station throughout the tunnel and will flash the number of the zone in which the stoppage has occurred. A red flashing pilot light will appear only at the signal control station at which the EMERGENCY TRUCK button was pressed. The emergency garage will receive an audible and visual signal indicating the signal control station at which the EMERGENCY TRUCK button was pressed. The garage officer shall acknowledge receipt of the signal by pressing the acknowledgment button. This will cause the pilot light at the operated signal control station in the tunnel to cease flashing and to remain steady. It is an answer to the officer at the operated signal control station that the emergency truck is responding to the call.

24. According to this paragraph, when the EMERGENCY TRUCK light button is pressed,

　　A. amber lights will go on in every lane throughout the tunnel
　　B. emergency signal lights will go on only in the lane in which the disabled vehicle happens to be
　　C. red lights will go on in the fast lane throughout the tunnel
　　D. pilot lights at all signal control stations will turn amber

25. According to this paragraph, the number of the zone in which the stoppage has occurred is flashed

　　A. immediately after all the lights in the tunnel turn red
　　B. by the yellow zone light at each signal control station
　　C. by the emergency truck at the point of stoppage
　　D. by the emergency garage

26. According to this paragraph, an officer near the disabled vehicle will know that the emergency tow truck is coming when

　　A. the pilot light at the operated signal control station appears and flashes red
　　B. an audible signal is heard in the tunnel

C. the zone light at the operated signal control station turns red
D. the pilot light at the operated signal control station becomes steady

27. Under the system described in the paragraph, it would be CORRECT to come to the conclusion that

   A. officers at all signal control stations are expected to acknowledge that they have received the stoppage signal
   B. officers at all signal control stations will know where the stoppage has occurred
   C. all traffic in both lanes of that side of the tunnel in which the stoppage has occurred must stop until the emergency truck has arrived
   D. there are two emergency garages, each able to respond to stoppages in traffic going in one particular direction

Questions 28-30.

DIRECTIONS: Answer questions 28 to 30 SOLELY on the basis of the following paragraphs.

In cases of accident, it is most important for an officer to obtain the name, age, residence, occupation, and a full description of the person injured, names and addresses of witnesses. He shall also obtain a statement of the attendant circumstances. He shall carefully note contributory conditions, if any, such as broken pavement, excavation, tights not burning, snow and ice on the roadway, etc. He shall enter all facts in his memorandum book and on Form 17 or Form 18 and promptly transmit the original of the form to his superior officer and the duplicate to headquarters.

An officer shall render reasonable assistance to sick or injured persons. If the circumstances appear to require the services of a physician, he shall summon a physician by telephoning the superior officer on duty and notifying him of the apparent nature of the illness or accident and the location where the physician will be required. He may summon other officers to assist if circumstances warrant.

In case of an accident or where a person is sick on city property, an officer shall obtain the information necessary to fill out card Form 18 and record this in his memorandum book and promptly telephone the facts to his superior officer. He shall deliver the original card at the expiration of his tour to his superior officer and transmit the duplicate to headquarters.

28. According to this quotation, the MOST important consideration in any report on a case of accident or injury is to

   A. obtain all the facts
   B. telephone his superior officer at once
   C. obtain a statement of the attendant circumstances
   D. determine ownership of the property on which the accident occurred

29. According to this quotation, in the case of an accident on city property, the officer should always

   A. summon a physician before filling out any forms or making any entries in his memorandum book
   B. give his superior officer on duty a prompt report by telephone

C. immediately bring the original of Form 18 to his superior officer on duty
D. call at least one other officer to the scene to witness conditions

30. If the procedures stated in this quotation were followed for all accidents in the city, an impartial survey of accidents occurring during any period of time in this city may be MOST easily made by

    A. asking a typical officer to show you his memorandum book
    B. having a superior officer investigate whether contributory conditions mentioned by witnesses actually exist
    C. checking all the records of all superior officers
    D. checking the duplicate card files at headquarters

Questions 31-55.

DIRECTIONS: In each of questions 31 to 55, select the lettered word or phrase which means MOST NEARLY the same as the first word in the row.

31. RENDEZVOUS

    A. parade   B. neighborhood
    C. meeting place   D. wander about

32. EMINENT

    A. noted   B. rich   C. rounded   D. nearby

33. CAUSTIC

    A. cheap   B. sweet   C. evil   D. sharp

34. BARTER

    A. annoy   B. trade   C. argue   D. cheat

35. APTITUDE

    A. friendliness   B. talent
    C. conceit   D. generosity

36. PROTRUDE

    A. project   B. defend   C. choke   D. boast

37. FORTITUDE

    A. disposition   B. restlessness
    C. courage   D. poverty

38. PRELUDE

    A. introduction   B. meaning
    C. prayer   D. secret

39. SECLUSION

    A. primitive   B. influence
    C. imagination   D. privacy

40. RECTIFY 40.____
    A. correct   B. construct   C. divide   D. scold

41. TRAVERSE 41.____
    A. rotate   B. compose   C. train   D. cross

42. ALLEGE 42.____
    A. raise   B. convict   C. declare   D. chase

43. MENIAL 43.____
    A. pleasant   B. unselfish
    C. humble   D. stupid

44. DEPLETE 44.____
    A. exhaust   B. gather   C. repay   D. close

45. ERADICATE 45.____
    A. construct   B. advise   C. destroy   D. exclaim

46. CAPITULATE 46.____
    A. cover   B. surrender   C. receive   D. execute

47. RESTRAIN 47.____
    A. restore   B. drive   C. review   D. limit

48. AMALGAMATE 48.____
    A. join   B. force   C. correct   D. clash

49. DEJECTED 49.____
    A. beaten   B. speechless
    C. weak   D. low-spirited

50. DETAIN 50.____
    A. hide   B. accuse   C. hold   D. mislead

KEY (CORRECT ANSWERS)

1. A	11. B	21. B	31. C	41. D
2. C	12. D	22. C	32. A	42. C
3. B	13. A	23. A	33. D	43. C
4. C	14. C	24. C	34. B	44. A
5. D	15. D	25. B	35. B	45. C
6. A	16. C	26. D	36. A	46. B
7. B	17. D	27. B	37. C	47. D
8. A	18. B	28. A	38. A	48. A
9. A	19. A	29. B	39. D	49. D
10. C	20. D	30. D	40. A	50. C

TEST 2

DIRECTIONS: Each question or incomplete statement is followed by several suggested answers or completions. Select the one that BEST answers the question or completes the statement. *PRINT THE LETTER OF THE CORRECT ANSWER IN THE SPACE AT THE RIGHT.*

1. AMPLE   1.____
    A. necessary   B. plentiful   C. protected   D. tasty

2. EXPEDITE   2.____
    A. sue   B. omit   C. hasten   D. verify

3. FRAGMENT   3.____
    A. simple tool   B. broken part
    C. basic outline   D. weakness

4. ADVERSARY   4.____
    A. thief   B. partner   C. loser   D. foe

5. ACHIEVE   5.____
    A. accomplish   B. begin   C. develop   D. urge

Questions 6-10.

DIRECTIONS: Answer Questions 6 to 10 on the basis of the information given in the table on the following page. The numbers which have been omitted from the table can be calculated from the other numbers which are given.

NUMBER OF DWELLING UNITS CONSTRUCTED

Year	Private one-family houses	In private apt. houses	In public housing	Total dwelling units
1996	4,500	500	600	5,600
1997	9,200	5,300	2,800	17,300
1998	8,900	12,800	6,800	28,500
1999	12,100	15,500	7,100	34,700
2000	?	12,200	14,100	39,200
2001	10,200	26,000	8,600	44,800
2002	10,300	17,900	7,400	35,600
2003	11,800	18,900	7,700	38,400
2004	12,700	22,100	8,400	43,200
2005	13,300	24,300	8,100	45,700
TOTALS	105,900	?	?	?

6. According to this table, the average number of public housing units constructed yearly during the period 1996 through 2005 was   6.____
    A. 7,160   B. 6,180   C. 7,610   D. 6,810

81

7. Of the following, the two years in which the number of private one-family homes constructed was GREATEST for the two years together is

   A. 1998 and 1999
   B. 1997 and 2003
   C. 1998 and 2004
   D. 2001 and 2002

8. For the entire period of 1996 through 2005, the total of all private one-family houses constructed exceeded the total of all public housing units constructed by

   A. 34,300
   B. 45,700
   C. 50,000
   D. 83,900

9. Of the total number of private apartment house dwelling units constructed in the ten years given in the table, the percentage which was constructed in 2002 was MOST NEARLY

   A. 5%
   B. 11%
   C. 16%
   D. 21%

10. Considering dwelling units of all types, the average number constructed annually in the period from 2001 through 2005 was GREATER than the average number constructed annually in the period from 1996 through 2000 by

    A. 16,480
    B. 33,320
    C. 79,300
    D. 82,400

11. A car speeds through the toll entrance of a 2 1/4 mile long bridge without paying the toll and reaches the other end of the bridge 1 minute and 30 seconds later. The car was traveling MOST NEARLY at a rate of _____ miles per hour.

    A. 60
    B. 70
    C. 80
    D. 90

12. During one week, 21,500 vehicles passed through the toll booths of a certain bridge. Of these, 550 were buses, 2,230 were trucks, and the rest were passenger cars. The toll charges were $3.50 for a passenger car, $7 for a truck and $14 for a bus. The total income for the week was

    A. $80,850
    B. $88,830
    C. $102,550
    D. $109,550

13. A bullet fired from a revolver travels 100 feet the first second, and each succeeding second it travels a distance 10% less than during the immediately preceding second. The number of feet the bullet will have traveled at the end of the fourth second is MOST NEARLY

    A. 272
    B. 320
    C. 344
    D. 360

14. An officer receives a uniform allowance of $500 a year in a lump sum. Of this amount, he spends $180 for a winter jacket and 40% of the remainder for two pairs of trousers. The officer now wishes to buy a winter overcoat which costs $240.
    The percentage of the purchase price of the overcoat by which he will be short is

    A. 20%
    B. 25%
    C. 48%
    D. 60%

15. It has been suggested that small light cars can be used for certain kinds of police work. These light vehicles can run 30 miles per gallon of gasoline as contrasted with standard cars which run only 15 miles per gallon. Assume gasoline costs the city $3.75 per gallon. During 9,000 miles of travel, use of the small light car in preference to the standard car would result in a saving in gasoline costs of MOST NEARLY

    A. $1,125
    B. $1,500
    C. $1,875
    D. $2,250

3 (#2)

16. Out of a total of 34,750 felony complaints in 2006, 14,200 involved burglary. In 2005, there was a total of 32,300 felony complaints of which 12,800 were burglary.
Of the increase in felonies from 2005 to 2006, the increase in burglaries comprised APPROXIMATELY

   A. 27%   B. 37%   C. 47%   D. 57%

17. A certain city department has two offices which issue permits, one office handling twice as many applicants as the other. The smaller office grants permits to 40% of its applicants. The larger office handling twice as many applicants grants permits to 60% of its applicants.
If there were 900 applicants at both offices together on a given day, the total number of permits granted by both offices would be MOST NEARLY

   A. 420   B. 450   C. 480   D. 510

18. If a co-worker is not breathing after receiving an electric shock but is no longer in contact with the electricity, it is MOST important for you to

   A. avoid moving him
   B. wrap the victim in a blanket
   C. start artificial respiration promptly
   D. force him to take hot liquids

19. Employees using supplies from one of the first-aid kits available throughout the building are required to submit an immediate report of the occurrence.
Logical reasoning shows that the MOST important reason for this report is so that the

   A. supplies used will be sure to be replaced
   B. first-aid kit can be properly sealed again
   C. employee will be credited for his action
   D. record of first-aid supplies will be up-to-date

20. The BEST IMMEDIATE first-aid treatment for a scraped knee is to

   A. apply plain vaseline   B. wash it with soap and water
   C. apply heat   D. use a knee splint

21. Artificial respiration after a severe electrical shock is ALWAYS necessary when the shock results in

   A. unconsciousness   B. stoppage of breathing
   C. bleeding   D. a burn

22. The authority gives some of its maintenance employees instruction in first aid.
The MOST likely reason for doing this is to

   A. eliminate the need for calling a doctor in case of accident
   B. provide temporary emergency treatment in case of accident
   C. lower the cost of accidents to the authority
   D. reduce the number of accidents

23. The BEST IMMEDIATE first aid if a chemical solution splashes into the eyes is to

   A. protect the eyes from the light by bandaging
   B. rub the eyes dry with a towel

C. cause tears to flow by staring at a bright light
D. flush the eyes with large quantities of clean water

24. If you had to telephone for an ambulance because of an accident, the MOST important information for you to give the person who answered the telephone would be the

   A. exact time of the accident
   B. cause of the accident
   C. place where the ambulance is needed
   D. names and addresses of those injured

25. If a person has a deep puncture wound in his finger caused by a sharp nail, the BEST IMMEDIATE first aid procedure would be to

   A. encourage bleeding by exerting pressure around the injured area
   B. stop all bleeding
   C. prevent air from reaching the wound
   D. probe the wound for steel particles

26. In addition to cases of submersion, artificial respiration is a recommended first aid procedure for

   A. sunstroke   B. electrical shock   C. chemical poisoning   D. apoplexy

27. Assume that you are called on to render first aid to a man injured in an accident. You find he is bleeding profusely, is unconscious, and has a broken arm. There is a strong odor of alcohol about him.
The FIRST thing for which you should treat him is the

   A. bleeding   B. unconsciousness   C. broken arm   D. alcoholism

28. In applying first aid for removal of a foreign body in the eye, an important precaution to be observed is NOT to

   A. attempt to wash out the foreign body
   B. bring the upper eyelid down over the lower
   C. rub the eye
   D. touch or attempt to remove a speck on the lower lid

29. The one of the following symptoms which is LEAST likely to indicate that a person involved in an accident requires first aid for shock is that

   A. he has fainted twice
   B. his face is red and flushed
   C. his skin is wet with sweat
   D. his pulse is rapid

30. When giving first aid to a person suffering from shock as a result of an auto accident, it is MOST important to

   A. massage him in order to aid blood circulation
   B. have him sip whiskey
   C. prop him up in a sitting position
   D. cover the person and keep him warm

Questions 31-34.

DIRECTIONS: Answer questions 31 to 34 SOLELY on the basis of the following paragraph.

Assume that you are an officer assigned to one large office which issues and receives applications for various permits and licenses. The office consists of one section where the necessary forms are issued; another section where fees are paid to a cashier; and desks where applicants are interviewed and their forms reviewed and completed. There is also a section containing tables and chairs where persons may sit and fill out their applications before being interviewed or paying the fees. your duties consist of answering simple questions, directing the public to the correct section of the office, and maintaining order.

31. A man who speaks English poorly asks you for assistance in obtaining and filling out an application for a permit. You should

    A. send him to an interviewer who can assist him
    B. try to determine what permit he wants and fill out the form for him
    C. refer the man to the office supervisor
    D. ask another applicant to help this person

31._____

32. The office becomes noisy and crowded, with people milling around waiting for service at the various sections.
Of the following, the BEST action for you to take is to

    A. stand in a prominent place and in a loud voice request the people to be quiet
    B. direct all the people not being served to wait at the unoccupied tables until you call them
    C. line up the people in front of each section and keep the lines in good order
    D. tell the people to form a single line outside the office and let in a few at a time

32._____

33. A man who has just been denied a permit becomes angry and shouts that if he "knew the right people" he too could get a permit. His behavior is disturbing the office.
Of the following, the BEST action for you to take is to

    A. order the man to leave at once since his business is done
    B. tell the man to be quiet and file another application
    C. suggest to the supervisor that a pamphlet be prepared explaining the requirements for permits in simple language
    D. ask an interviewer to explain the requirements for his permit to the person and his right of appeal

33._____

34. Just before the close of business, a man rushes in and insists on being interviewed for a permit because his present one expires that night.
Of the following, the BEST action for you to take is to

    A. tell the man that the office is closed
    B. tell the man that there will be no penalty if he returns early the next morning
    C. inquire if an interviewer is still available to take care of him and send him to that desk
    D. tell the cashier to collect the fee and tell the man to return the next morning for an interview

34._____

35. Fingerprints are often taken of applicants for licenses. Of the following, the MOST valid reason for this procedure is that

    A. the license of someone who commits a crime can be more readily revoked
    B. applicants can be checked for possible criminal records
    C. it helps to make sure that the proper license fee is paid
    D. a complete employment record of the applicant is obtained

36. Assume that an officer is on patrol at 2 A.M. He notices that the night light inside one of the stores in a public building is out. The store is locked.
    Of the following, the FIRST action for him to take at this time is to

    A. continue on his patrol since the light probably burned out
    B. enter the store by any means possible so he can check it
    C. report the matter to his superior
    D. shine his flashlight through the window to look for anything unusual

37. In questioning a man suspected of having committed a theft, the BEST procedure for an officer to follow is to

    A. induce the man to express his feelings about the police, the courts, and his home environment
    B. threaten him with beatings when he refuses to answer your questions
    C. make any promises necessary to get him to confess
    D. remain calm and objective

38. As an officer, you are on duty in one of the offices of a large public building. A woman who has just finished her business with this office comes to you and reports that her son who was with her is missing.
    The one of the following which is the BEST action for you to take FIRST is to

    A. tell the mother that the child is probably all right and ask her to go to the local police station for help in finding the boy
    B. suggest that the mother wait in the office until the child turns up
    C. check nearby offices in an attempt to locate the child
    D. telephone the local police station and ask if any reports fitting the description of the child have been received

39. An officer assigned to patrol inside a public building at night has observed two men standing outside the doorway. Of the following, the MOST appropriate action for the officer to take FIRST is to

    A. approach the two men and ask them why they are standing there
    B. hide and wait for the two men to take some action
    C. phone the local police station and ask for help since these men may be planning criminal action
    D. check all the entrance doors of the building to make sure that they are locked

40. It is standard practice for special officers to inspect the restrooms in public buildings. This is done at regular intervals while on patrol.
    Of the following, the BEST reason for this practice is to

    A. inspect sanitary conditions
    B. discourage loiterers and potential criminals

C. check the ventilation
D. determine if all the equipment and plumbing is working properly

41. While on duty in the evening as an officer assigned to a public building, you receive a report that a card game is going on in one of the offices. Gambling is forbidden on government property.
Of the following, the BEST course of action for you to take is to

    A. go to the office and order the card players to leave
    B. ignore the complaint since this is probably just harmless social card playing
    C. report the matter to the building manager the next day
    D. go to the office and, if warranted, issue an appropriate warning

41.____

42. It has been suggested that special officers establish good working relationships with the local police officers of the police department on duty in the neighborhood.
Of the following, the MOST valid reason for this practice is that

    A. a spirit of good feeling and high morale will be created among members of the police department
    B. local police officers will probably cooperate more readily with the special officer
    C. local police officers can take over the building patrol duties of the special officer in case he is absent
    D. special officers have an even stronger obligation than ordinary citizens to cooperate with the police

42.____

43. It has been proposed that an officer assigned to a public building at night remain at one location in the building, instead of walking on patrol through the building.
This proposal is

    A. *bad;* chiefly because the officer would probably sit instead of stand at the proper location
    B. *good;* chiefly because the officer could do a better job of watching the entire building from one point
    C. *bad;* chiefly because anyone seeking to enter the building for illegal purposes might be able to do so at a point other than where the special officer is on duty
    D. *good;* chiefly because his supervisors would know exactly where to find him

43.____

44. In a busy office, an officer has been assigned the duty of making sure that the public is served in the order of their arrival at the office and that some employee is always taking care of a person desiring help.
Of the following, the BEST method for the officer to follow is to

    A. line up the persons in the waiting room
    B. give a numbered ticket to each person waiting and call out the numbers, in order, when an employee becomes available
    C. loudly announce "next" when an employee is available to serve someone
    D. seat one person next to each employee's desk and let the others wait for the first vacant seat

44.____

45. Two men have broken into and entered a building at night. The officer on duty at this building sees them, chases them out, and then observes them in the adjoining building.
Of the following, the BEST course of action for the officer to take is to

   A. notify the local police station and be ready to aid the police
   B. enter the adjoining building to find the men
   C. notify the manager of his own building
   D. continue on duty since these men have left the building for which he is responsible

46. While an officer is on duty in a crowded waiting room, he finds a woman's purse on the floor.
Of the following, the FIRST course of action for him to take is to

   A. hold it up in the air, ask who owns it, and give it to whoever claims it
   B. keep the purse until someone claims it
   C. immediately deliver the purse to the "lost and found" desk
   D. ask the lady who is nearest to him if she lost a purse

47. Special officers often have the power of arrest.
Of the following, the BEST reason for this practice is to

   A. have the officer always arrest any person who refuses to obey his orders
   B. aid in maintaining order in places where he is assigned
   C. promote good public relations
   D. aid in preventing illegal use of public buildings by tenants or employees

48. An officer has told a mother that he found her son writing on the walls of the building with chalk. The mother tells the officer that he should be more concerned with "crooks" than with children's minor pranks.
Of the following, the BEST answer for the officer to make to this woman is that

   A. children should be taught good conduct by their parents
   B. damage to public property means higher taxes
   C. serious criminals often begin their careers with minor violations
   D. it is his duty to enforce all rules and regulations

49. A man asks you, a special officer, where to get a certain kind of license not issued in your office. You don't know where such licenses are issued.
Of the following, the BEST procedure for you to follow is to

   A. refer him to the manager of the office
   B. get the information if you can and give it to the man
   C. tell the man to inquire at any police station house
   D. tell the man that you just do not know

50. Special officers are not permitted to ask private citizens to buy tickets for dances or other such social functions, not even when such functions are operated by charitable organizations. Of the following, the BEST reason for this rule is that

   A. private citizens are under no obligation to buy any such tickets
   B. not all groups are allowed equal opportunity in the sale of their tickets
   C. private citizens might complain to officials
   D. private citizens might feel they would not get proper service unless they bought such tickets

KEY (CORRECT ANSWERS)

1. B	11. D	21. B	31. A	41. D
2. C	12. B	22. B	32. C	42. B
3. B	13. C	23. D	33. D	43. C
4. D	14. A	24. C	34. C	44. B
5. A	15. A	25. A	35. B	45. A
6. A	16. D	26. B	36. D	46. C
7. C	17. C	27. A	37. D	47. B
8. A	18. C	28. C	38. C	48. D
9. B	19. A	29. B	39. D	49. B
10. A	20. B	30. D	40. B	50. D

SOLUTIONS TO ARITHMETIC PROBLEMS

11. $2\frac{1}{4}$ miles are completed in 1 1/2 minutes (1 minute and 30 seconds)

   $\therefore 2\frac{1}{4} \div 1\frac{1}{2}$ = rate per minute

   $= \frac{9}{4} \div 1\frac{1}{2}$

   $= \frac{9}{4} \div \frac{3}{2}$

   $= \frac{9}{4} \times \frac{2}{3}$

   $= \frac{3}{2}$ miles per minute

   $\therefore \frac{3}{2} \times 60$ (minutes in an hour) = rate per hour = 90 miles per hour

   (Ans. D)

12. 550 + 2230 = 2780; 21,500 - 2780 = 18,720 passengers

550 buses at $14.00	=	$ 7,700
2230 trucks at $7.00	=	15,610
18720 passengers at $3.50	=	65,520
		$88,830

    (Ans. B)

13. Given: speed = 100 feet the first second

100 - 10 (10% of 100)	=	90 feet - the second second
90 - 9 (10% of 90)	=	81 feet - the third second
81 - 8.1 (10% of 81)	=	72.9 feet - the fourth second
		343.9 (total at end of the fourth second)

    (Ans. C)

14. Given: 500 = uniform allowance

    $500 - 180 = $320   (amount left after buying winter jacket)
    $320 x 40% = $128   (amount spent for two pairs of trousers)
    $320 - 128 = $192   (amount now left)

    Since the winter overcoat costs $240, he is now short $48 ($240 - 192) or 20% of the purchase price of the overcoat. (48/240 = $\frac{1}{5}$ = 20%)

(Ans. A)

15. Light care: 9000(miles)÷30(miles per gallon)×3.75(per gallon)

$$=\frac{9000}{30} \times 3.75$$
$$= 300 \times 3.75$$
$$= \$1,125 \text{ (total gasoline cost)}$$

Standard cars: 9000 (miles) ÷ 15 (miles per gallon) x 3.75

$$=\frac{9000}{15} \times 3.75$$
$$= 600 \times 3.75$$
$$= \$2,250 \text{ (total gasoline cost)}$$

∴ use of light car would result in a saving in gasoline costs of $1,125 ($2,250 - $1,125).

(Ans. A)

16. 2006: 14,200 (burglary)
     2005: 12,800 (burglary)
            1,400   (increase in burglaries)

     2006: 34,750 (felony)
     2005: 32,300 (felony)
            2,450   (increase in felonies

$$\therefore 1400 \div 2450 = \frac{1400}{2450} = .57$$

WORK

```
          .57
    2450)1400.0
         1225.0
          175.00
          171.50
```

(Ans. D)

17. Given: smaller office: grants permits to 40% of 1/3 of the total number of applicants (900)

    larger office: grants permits to 60% of 2/3 of the total number of applicants (900)

    Solving: smaller office: $.40 \times \frac{1}{3} \times 900 = 120$ permits

    larger office: $.60 \times \frac{2}{3} \times 900 = \underline{360}$ permits
    $\phantom{larger office: .60 \times \frac{2}{3} \times 900 = }\overline{480}$ permits (total)

(Ans. C)

EXAMINATION SECTION
TEST 1

DIRECTIONS: Each question or incomplete statement is followed by several suggested answers or completions. Select the one that BEST answers the question or completes the statement. *PRINT THE LETTER OF THE CORRECT ANSWER IN THE SPACE AT THE RIGHT.*

Questions 1-9.

DIRECTIONS: Questions 1 through 9 are to be answered SOLELY on the basis of the following information and the DIRECTORY OF SERVICES.

Officer Johnson has just been assigned to the North End Service Facility and is now on his post in the main lobby. The facility is open to the public from 9 A.M. to 5 P.M. each Monday through Friday, except on Thursdays when it is open from 9 A.M. to 7 P.M. The facility is closed on holidays.

Officer Johnson must ensure an orderly flow of visitors through the lobby of the facility. To accomplish this, Officer Johnson gives directions and provides routine information to clients and other members of the public who enter and leave the facility through the lobby.

In order to give directions and provide routine information to visitors, such as information concerning the location of services, Officer Johnson consults the Directory of Services shown below. Officer Johnson must ensure that clients are directed to the correct room for service and are sent to that room only during the hours that the particular service is available. When clients ask for the location of more than one service, they should be directed to go first to the service that will close soonest.

NORTH END SERVICE FACILITY
DIRECTORY OF SERVICES

Room	Type of Service	Days Available	Hours Open
101	Facility Receptionist	Monday, Tuesday, Wednesday, Friday	9 AM- 5 PM
		Thursday	9 AM- 7 PM
103	Photo Identification Cards	Monday, Wednesday, Friday	9 AM-12 Noon
104	Lost and Stolen Identification Cards	Wednesday, Thursday	9 AM-5 PM
105	Applications for Welfare/Food Stamps	Wednesday, Friday	1 PM-5 PM
107	Recertification for Welfare/Food Stamps	Monday, Thursday	10 AM- 12 Noon
108	Medicaid Applications	Tuesday, Wednesday	2 PM-5 PM
109	Medicaid Complaints	Tuesday, Wednesday	10 AM-2 PM
110, 111	Social Worker	Monday, Wednesday	9 AM-12 Noon
		Tuesday, Friday	1 PM-5 PM
		Thursday	9 AM- 5 PM
114	Hearing Room (By appointment only)	Monday, Thursday	9 AM-5 PM

DIRECTORY OF SERVICES
(CONT'D)

Room	Type of Service	Days Available	Hours Open
115	Hearing Information	Monday, Tuesday, Wednesday, Thursday, Friday	9 AM-1 PM
206, 207	Nutrition Aid	Monday, Wednesday, Friday	10 AM-2 PM
		Tuesday, Thursday	9 AM-12 Noon
215	Health Clinic	Monday, Tuesday, Wednesday, Friday	9 AM-5 PM
		Thursday	9 AM-7 PM
220	Facility Administrative Office	Monday, Tuesday, Wednesday, Thursday, Friday	9 AM-5 PM

1. It is Tuesday morning and Ms. Loretta Rogers, a client of the North End Service Facility, asks Officer Johnson where she should go in order to apply for Medicaid. Officer Johnson tells Ms. Rogers to go to Room _____ at _____.

    A. 108; 1:00 P.M.
    B. 109; 11:00 A.M.
    C. 108; 2:00 P.M.
    D. 109; 2:00 P.M.

2. On Friday at 11:00 A.M., Mrs. Ruth Ramos, a new client at the North End Service Facility, tells Officer Johnson that she wants to obtain a photo identification card and see a social worker.
Officer Johnson should direct Mrs. Ramos to first go to Room

    A. 103   B. 104   C. 110   D. 220

3. On Friday at 10:30 A.M., a client at the North End Service Facility who is directed by Officer Johnson to go to Room 206 will be able to receive service regarding

    A. Recertification for Welfare/Food Stamps
    B. Hearing Information
    C. Medicaid Applications
    D. Nutrition Aid

4. At 9:00 A.M. on Monday, a client at the North End Service Facility who is directed by Officer Johnson to Room 101 for service will find

    A. Nutrition Aid
    B. Facility Receptionist
    C. Health Clinic
    D. Hearing Information

5. On Tuesday at 12:30 P.M., Mr. Paul Brown tells Officer Johnson that he lost his identification card and wants to obtain a new one as soon as possible.
Officer Johnson should direct Mr. Brown to go to Room 104

    A. immediately
    B. at 1:00 P.M. that day
    C. at 9:00 A.M. on Wednesday
    D. at 2:00 P.M. on Friday

6. A client at the North End Service Facility explains to Officer Johnson that he wants to make an appointment with a Social Worker.
   The client should be directed to go to Room

   A. 104   B. 110   C. 115   D. 215

7. Ms. Alice Lee is a client at the North End Service Facility who has a 10:00 A.M. appointment on Thursday in the Hearing Room and does not know where to go.
   Officer Johnson should direct Ms. Lee to go to Room

   A. 101   B. 110   C. 112   D. 114

8. Officer Johnson is asked by a visitor which services are available on Thursdays between 5:00 P.M. and 7:00 P.M. Officer Johnson should inform the visitor that an available service during that time is

   A. Health Clinic
   B. Medicaid Complaints
   C. Nutrition Aid
   D. Social Worker

9. Mr. Jack Klein, a visitor to the North End Service Facility, asks Officer Johnson when and where he can file a complaint concerning Medicaid.
   Officer Johnson should inform Mr. Klein that he may go to Room

   A. 108 on Tuesday or Wednesday between 2:00 P.M. and 5:00 P.M.
   B. 109 on Tuesday or Wednesday between 10:00 A.M. and 2:00 P.M.
   C. 115 on Monday or Tuesday between 10:00 A.M. and 12:00 Noon
   D. 215 on Thursday between 9:00 A.M. and 7:00 P.M.

Questions 10-12.

DIRECTIONS: Questions 10 through 12 are to be answered SOLELY on the basis of the following information.

Security Officers should act in accordance with guidelines included in a manual provided to security staff. Assume that the following guidelines apply to Officers when in contact with visitors or clients in a facility:

1. Try to see things from the visitor's or client's point of view.
2. Ignore insulting comments.
3. Maintain a calm and patient manner.
4. Speak quietly, courteously, and tactfully.

10. Officer Renee Williams is patrolling the lobby area of her facility when she hears a client angrily yelling at the receptionist. She goes to investigate the situation and finds out from the receptionist that the client is one hour late for his appointment with a social worker who now has other appointments. The client demands to be seen by the social worker immediately. Officer Williams angrily tells the client that it is his own fault that he missed his appointment and he should stop bothering the receptionist and go home.
    In this situation, Officer Williams' behavior towards the client is

    A. *proper,* chiefly because it is the client's fault that he missed his appointment
    B. *improper,* chiefly because security officers should stay calm and speak courteously when dealing with clients
    C. *proper,* chiefly because the client had yelled at the receptionist
    D. *improper,* chiefly because the security officer should have ignored the whole incident

11. During his tour, Officer Montgomery is passing through his facility's waiting room on the way to the cafeteria for a break. As Officer Montgomery passes by a visitor, the visitor mutters an insulting remark about the Officer's appearance. Officer Montgomery ignores the visitor and the remark and proceeds on his way to the cafeteria.
Officer Montgomery's action in this situation is

    A. *correct,* chiefly because it is not necessary for Officer Montgomery to respond to visitors while on a break
    B. *incorrect,* chiefly because Officer Montgomery should have ejected the visitor from the facility
    C. *correct,* chiefly because special officers should ignore insults
    D. *incorrect,* chiefly because visitors should not be allowed to ridicule authority figures such as special officers

12. While patrolling the facility parking lot, Officer Klausner sees an unoccupied car parked in front of a fire hydrant. Officer Klausner writes out a summons for a parking violation and places it on the windshield of the car. As the Officer begins to walk away, the owner of the car spots the summons on the windshield and runs over to the car. The car owner is furious at getting the summons, confronts the Officer, and curses him loudly.
In this situation, Officer Klausner should

    A. curse back at the car owner just as loudly
    B. push him out of the way and resume patrol
    C. calmly explain to him the nature of the violation
    D. return all the insults but in a calm tone

Question 13.

DIRECTIONS: Question 13 is to be answered SOLELY on the basis of the following information.

Special Officers are permitted to give only general information about social services. They shall not provide advice concerning specific procedures.

13. Special Officer Lynn King is on post near the Medicaid Office in the Manhattan Income Maintenance Center. While Officer King is on post, a client approaches her and asks which forms must be filled out in order to apply for Medicaid benefits. Officer King tells the client that she cannot help him and directs the client to the Medicaid Office.
In this situation, Officer King's response to the client's question is

    A. *correct,* chiefly because Officer King's duties do not include providing any information to clients
    B. *incorrect,* chiefly because Officer King should have provided as much specific information as possible to the client
    C. *correct,* chiefly because Officer King may not advise clients on social services procedures
    D. *incorrect,* chiefly because Officer King should know which forms are used in the facility

Question 14.

DIRECTIONS: Question 14 is to be answered SOLELY on the basis of the following information.

Security Officers must request that visitors and clients show identification and inspect that identification before allowing them to enter restricted areas in the facility.

14. Security Officer Crane is assigned to a fixed post outside Commissioner Maxwell's office, which is a restricted area. A visitor approaches Officer Crane's desk and states that he is Robert Maxwell and has an appointment with the Commissioner, who is his brother. Officer Crane checks the appointment book, verifies that Robert Maxwell has an appointment with the Commissioner, and allows the visitor to enter the office.
In this situation, Officer Crane's action in allowing the visitor admittance to the Commissioner's office is

14.____

 A. *correct*, chiefly because he verified that Robert Maxwell had an appointment with the Commissioner
 B. *incorrect*, chiefly because all visitors must show identification before entering restricted areas
 C. *correct*, chiefly because it would insult the Commissioner's brother if he was asked to show identification
 D. *incorrect*, chiefly because he should have called the Commissioner to verify that he has a brother

Question 15.

DIRECTIONS: Question 15 is to be answered SOLELY on the basis of the following information.

While on duty, a Special Officer must give his rank, name, and shield number to any person who requests it.

15. Special Officer Karen Mitchell is assigned to patrol an area in the North Bronx Service Facility. While on patrol, Officer Mitchell observes a visitor asking other clients in the lobby for money. Upon investigation, she determines that the visitor has no official business in the facility and asks the visitor to leave the premises. The individual says that he will leave but demands to know Officer Mitchell's name and shield number.
In response to the visitor's demand, Officer Mitchell should

15.____

 A. give the individual her name and shield number
 B. inform him that he can only obtain that information from her supervisor
 C. ignore his demand and resume her patrol
 D. tell the visitor that she will issue a summons to him if he keeps bothering her

Question 16.

DIRECTIONS: Question 16 is to be answered SOLELY on the basis of the following information.

A member of the Security Staff must follow guidelines for providing information to reporters concerning official facility business. Special Officers shall not be interviewed, nor make public speeches or statements pertaining to official business unless authorized. Security Staff must receive authorization from the Office of Public Affairs before speaking to reporters on any matters pertaining to official facility business.

16. You are a Special Officer in a Men's Shelter. A reporter approaches you as you are leaving the building. The reporter requests that you give an insider's view on conditions in the shelter. He assures you that you will remain anonymous.
You should tell the reporter that you

A. must obtain permission from your immediate supervisor before giving any interviews
B. will be more than happy to provide him with information concerning conditions in the shelter
C. must receive authorization from the Office of Public Affairs before giving any interviews
D. may not give him any information, but that your supervisor will be able to provide him with the requested information.

Questions 17-21.

DIRECTIONS: Questions 17 through 21 are to be answered SOLELY on the basis of the following information.

During their tours, Security Officers are required to transmit and receive information and commands over two-way portable radios from other security staff members. Officers use a numbered code to transmit information over the radio. For example, an officer who calls *10-13* into his radio communicates to other officers and supervisors that he is in need of assistance. Assume that the code numbers shown below along with their specified meanings are those used by Special Officers.

Code	Meaning
10-01	Call your command
10-02	Report to your command
10-03	Call Dispatcher
10-04	Acknowledgment
10-05	Repeat message
10-06	Stand-by
10-07	Verify
10-08	Respond to specified area and advise
10-10	Investigate
10-13	Officer needs help
10-20	Robbery in progress
10-21	Burglary in progress
10-22	Larceny in progress
10-24	Assault in progress
10-30	Robbery has occurred

10-31	Burglary has occurred
10-34	Assault has occurred
10-40	Unusual incident
10-41	Vehicle accident
10-42	Traffic or parking problem
10-43	Electrical problem
10-50	Dispute or noise
10-52	Disorderly person/group
10-60	Ambulance needed
10-61	Police Department assistance required
10-64	Fire alarm
10-70	Arrived at scene
10-71	Arrest
10-72	Unfounded
10-73	Condition corrected
10-74	Resuming normal duties

17. Officer Cramer is patrolling Parking Lot A when he receives a radio message from Sergeant Wong. Sergeant Wong directs Officer Cramer to respond to Parking Lot B to investigate a reported traffic problem. Upon arriving at Parking Lot B, Officer Cramer observes a vehicle blocking a loading dock so that a delivery truck cannot gain access to the dock. After notification is made to the owner of the vehicle, the vehicle is moved, allowing the delivery truck to gain access to the loading dock. Which of the following should Officer Cramer use to BEST report the events that occurred back to Sergeant Wong?   17.____

   A. 10-72, 10-41, 10-73
   B. 10-70, 10-42, 10-73
   C. 10-70, 10-41, 10-74
   D. 10-72, 10-42, 10-74

18. Officer Garret receives a message of *10-24, 10-10* on his radio from his supervisor, Sergeant Gomez. Officer Garret responds to the scene and later sends Sergeant Gomez the following message in response: *10-70, 10-72, 10-74*. Which of the following events are reported by use of those codes?   18.____
Sergeant Gomez ordered Officer Garret to investigate an assault

   A. in progress. Officer Garret arrived at the scene, discovered that the report was unfounded, and resumed normal duties.
   B. that had occurred. Officer Garret arrived at the scene, made an arrest, and then resumed normal duties.
   C. that had occurred. Officer Garret arrived at the scene and discovered that the report was unfounded and resumed normal duties.
   D. in progress. Officer Garret arrived at the scene, made an arrest, and then resumed normal duties.

19. Officer Torres is patrolling the grounds of his facility when he receives a radio message from Sergeant Washington. In response to the radio message, Officer Torres goes to the facility's parking lot and issues a summons to a vehicle blocking an ambulance entrance. The radio message that Officer Torres received from Sergeant Washington is 10-10,

    A. 10-21   B. 10-40   C. 10-42   D. 10-43

20. Officer Oxford transmits the following codes by radio to Sergeant Joseph: *10-20, 10-13*. The response that Officer Oxford receives from Sergeant Joseph on her radio is *10-04*. Which one of the following events are reported by the use of those codes?
    Officer Oxford informed Sergeant Joseph that

    A. a robbery was in progress and that she needs assistance, and Sergeant Joseph acknowledged her message
    B. an assault was in progress and that she wants him to respond to the area, and Sergeant Joseph acknowledged her message
    C. a burglary was in progress and that someone must investigate, and Sergeant Joseph responded that he is standing by
    D. a larceny was in progress and that she needs him to call a dispatcher. Sergeant Joseph reports this incident to his command.

21. While on patrol, Officer Robinson observes that the hall lights in Wing *B* are flickering on and off. Officer Robinson calls the Maintenance Office and a maintenance worker responds and corrects the problem.
    The radio code that Officer Robinson should transmit to his supervisor to report this incident is

    A. 10-06,10-08   B. 10-40,10-64
    C. 10-43,10-73   D. 10-61,10-07

Question 22.

DIRECTIONS: Question 22 is to be answered SOLELY on the basis of the following information.

The two-way portable radios used by Security or Special Officers to communicate with other security staff members are to be used for official business only. In addition, when transmitting official business, transmission time (time spent transmitting information to other staff) should be kept to a minimum.

22. During his tour, Special Officer Banks calls Sergeant Gates in the patrolroom over the radio and asks if his wife, Alice Banks, had telephoned. Sergeant Gates tells Officer Banks that his wife has not called. Officer Banks then requests that Sergeant Gates notify him as soon as his wife calls because he is expecting an important message concerning his family.
    In this situation, Officer Banks' use of his radio is

    A. *appropriate,* chiefly because his transmission time was not excessive
    B. *inappropriate,* chiefly because he should have made the transmission on his break
    C. *appropriate,* chiefly because his transmission concerned an important family matter
    D. *inappropriate,* chiefly because radios are to be used for official business only

Question 23.

DIRECTIONS: Question 23 is to be answered SOLELY on the basis of the following information.

Special Officers are responsible for monitoring and responding to radio messages, even if the officer is on meal break, performing clerical duties, or away from his post for other reasons. An officer shall answer radio messages directed to him during his tour.

23. Officer Lewis is chatting with friends in the cafeteria while on her scheduled meal break when she receives a radio message from Sergeant Baker. Sergeant Baker informs Officer Lewis that trouble has broken out at Location A and directs her to report to Location A immediately to assist the officers on the scene. Officer Lewis leaves the cafeteria immediately and reports to the scene.
Officer Lewis' action in response to Sergeant Baker's radio message is

    A. *correct,* chiefly because Officer Lewis is responsible for responding to all radio messages
    B. *incorrect,* chiefly because Officer Lewis is on meal break and therefore *off-duty*
    C. *correct,* chiefly because Officer Lewis was not doing anything important during her meal break
    D. *incorrect,* chiefly because the situation was not declared a *total emergency*

Question 24.

DIRECTIONS: Question 24 is to be answered SOLELY on the basis of the following information.

Special Officers must immediately report to their supervisor any incident or condition in the facility that may cause danger or inconvenience to the public.

24. Special Officer Scott is patrolling a small, crowded waiting room in his facility when two male clients start arguing with each other, shoving chairs around and frightening the other clients. Officer Scott intervenes in the argument, issues summonses for Disorderly Conduct to the individuals involved in the dispute, and escorts them off the premises. Officer Scott then records the incident in his memo book and resumes patrol.
In this situation, the FIRST action that Officer Scott should have taken when he observed the argument start between the two men is to

    A. call for help from Special Officers on nearby posts to restrain the men who were fighting
    B. report the incident to his supervisor immediately
    C. attempt to separate the men who were fighting in order to stop the fight
    D. evacuate the waiting room so that innocent bystanders would not be injured

Question 25.

DIRECTIONS: Question 25 is to be answered SOLELY on the basis of the following information.

An Officer on duty in a facility must remain on post until properly relieved. If not properly relieved as scheduled, he must notify his immediate supervisor by radio of this fact and follow the supervisor's instructions.

25. Officer Clough is working on an 8:00 A.M. to 4:00 P.M. tour. Officer Clough is to be relieved at 4:00 P.M. by Security Officer Crandall, who works the 4:00 P.M. to 12:00 Midnight shift. However, as of 4:15 P.M., Officer Crandall has not appeared to relieve Officer Clough, so Officer Clough leaves his post to find Officer Crandall. In this situation, Officer Clough's action is

A. *correct,* chiefly because his tour was over and he wanted to go home
B. *incorrect,* chiefly because he should have notified his supervisor of Officer Crandall's failure to relieve him
C. *correct,* chiefly because Officer Clough is attempting to locate Officer Crandall so that the post will be covered
D. *incorrect,* chiefly because Officer Clough should have left his post as soon as his tour ended rather than working any overtime

Questions 26-28.

DIRECTIONS: Questions 26 through 28 are to be answered SOLELY on the basis of the following information.

A summons is a written notice that a person is accused of violating a code or regulation. Special Officers have the authority to issue summonses to individuals for on-premises parking or traffic violations, or violations of the City Administrative Code. Summonses for violations of the Penal Law, such as for Disorderly Conduct, may also be issued.

The following is a list of types of summonses issued for violations and their descriptions:

Type of Summons	Description of Violation
Class A	Parking in fire lanes
Class A	Parking in space reserved for the handicapped
Class A	Vehicle blocking driveway
Class B	Disobeying stop sign
Class C	Disorderly Conduct
Class C	Harassment
Environmental Control Board	Smoking Violations
Environmental Control Board	Public Health Code

26. While on patrol, Special Officer Gladys Jones observes a parked car that is blocking a driveway.
She should issue a summons for a violation which is a

A. Class A type
B. Class B type
C. Class C type
D. Environmental Control Board

27. A man drives up to a facility, parks his car in a fire lane, and quickly runs inside the facility. An attempt to follow and locate the man is unsuccessful.
Which one of the following is the type of summons that the Special Officer on duty should issue?

    A. Class A   B. Class B
    C. Class C   D. Environmental Control Board

27.____

28. While on patrol, Special Officer Mason observes a visitor smoking a cigarette in an area where smoking is prohibited. Officer Mason asks the visitor to stop smoking and shows him the *No Smoking* sign posted. The visitor refuses to comply.
Officer Mason should issue which type of summons?

    A. Class A   B. Class B
    C. Class C   D. Environmental Control Board

28.____

Questions 29-31.

DIRECTIONS: Questions 29 through 31 are to be answered SOLELY on the basis of the following information and the Summons Form and Fact Pattern.

Special Officers must complete a summons form by filling in the appropriate information. A completed summons must include the name and address of the accused; license or other identification number; vehicle identification; the section number of the code, regulation, or law violated; a brief description of the violation; any scheduled fine; information about the time and place of occurrence; and the name, rank, and signature of the Special Officer issuing the summons.

The information listed on the Summons Form may or may not be correct.

SUMMONS FORM

LINE				
1	NOTICE OF VIOLATION No. 5 56784989	THE PEOPLE OF THE STATE OF NEW YORK VS. _____ OPERATOR PRESENT NO (YES) REFUSED ID		
2	LAST NAME *Tucker*	FIRST NAME *James*	MIDDLE INITIAL *T*	
3	STREET ADDRESS *205 E. 53rd Street*			
4	CITY (AS SHOWN ON LICENSE) *Brooklyn, NY 11234*			
5	DRIVER LICENSE OR IDENTIFICATION NO. *J-7156907834*	STATE *NY*	CLASS *5*	DATE EXPIRES *1/12/13*
6	SEX *M*	DATE OF BIRTH *1/12/65*		
7	LICENSE PLATE NO. *CVR-632*	STATE *NY*	DATE EXPIRES *8/12/12*	OPERATOR OWN VEHICLE? (YES) NO
8	BODY TYPE *Sedan*	MAKE *Dodge*	COLOR *Green*	
	THE PERSON DESCRIBED ABOVE IS CHARGED AS FOLLOWS:			
9	ISSUE TIME *9:30 A.M.*	DATE OF OFFENSE *2/5/12*	TIME FIRST OBSERVED *9:28 A.M.*	COUNTY *Kings*
10	PLACE OF OCCURRENCE *451 Clarkson Ave., Brooklyn, NY*		PRECINCT *71st*	
11	IN VIOLATION OF SECTION *81-B*	CODE *40*	LAW *New York State Traffic Regulation*	
12	DESCRIPTION OF VIOLATION *Vehicle parked in front of a fire hydrant*			
13	SCHEDULED FINE $10 $15 $20 $25 $30 ($40) Other $____			
14	RANK/NAME OF ISSUING OFFICER *Special Officer Joseph Robbins*		SIGNATURE OF ISSUING OFFICER *Joseph Robbins*	

FACT PATTERN

On February 5, 2012, at 9:28 A.M., Special Officer Joseph Robbins is patrolling the grounds of the Brooklyn Hills Income Maintenance Center, located at 451 Clarkson Ave., Brooklyn, NY, when he observes an unoccupied parked vehicle blocking a fire hydrant near the facility's entrance. As Officer Robbins begins to write up a summons for the violation, James Tucker, the owner of the vehicle, emerges from the facility and comes over. While getting in his car, he asks why he is getting a summons. Officer Robbins explains to Mr. Tucker that he is in violation of traffic regulations pertaining to access to fire hydrants and asks him for identification. Mr. Tucker gives Officer Robbins his driver's license, showing the following information:

Name:	Tucker, James T.
Address:	205 E. 53rd Street, Brooklyn, NY 11234
Date of Birth:	January 12, 1965
Driver's License:	J-7156907894
Driver License Expiration Date:	January 12, 2013
Class:	5

29. The *place of occurrence* of the violation described in the Fact Pattern is on line _____ of the Summons Form.

    A. 2 B. 3 C. 8 D. 10

30. Which one of the following lines on the Summons Form shows information that does NOT agree with information given in the Fact Pattern?

    A. 1 B. 2 C. 4 D. 5

31. Which of the following is the date on which the violation occurred?

    A. 1/12/12 B. 2/5/12 C. 8/12/12 D. 1/12/13

32. Following are two sentences which may or may not be written in correct English:
    I. Two clients assaulted the officer.
    II. The van is illegally parked.
    Which one of the following statements is CORRECT?

    A. Only Sentence I is written in correct English.
    B. Only Sentence II is written in correct English.
    C. Sentences I and II are both written in correct English.
    D. Neither Sentence I nor Sentence II is written in correct English.

33. Following are two sentences which may or may not be written in correct English:
    I. Security Officer Rollo escorted the visitor to the patrolroom.
    II. Two entry were made in the facility logbook.
    Which one of the following statements is CORRECT?

    A. Only Sentence I is written in correct English.
    B. Only Sentence II is written in correct English.
    C. Sentences I and II are both written in correct English.
    D. Neither Sentence I nor Sentence II is written in correct English.

34. Following are two sentences which may or may not be written in correct English:
    I. Officer McElroy putted out a small fire in the wastepaper basket.
    II. Special Officer Janssen told the visitor where he could obtained a pass.
Which one of the following statements is CORRECT?

   A. Only Sentence I is written in correct English.
   B. Only Sentence II is written in correct English.
   C. Sentences I and II are both written in correct English.
   D. Neither Sentence I nor Sentence II are written in correct English.

35. Following are two sentences which may or may not be written in correct English:
    I. Security Officer Warren observed a broken window while he was on his post in Hallway C.
    II. The worker reported that two typewriters had been stoled from the office.
Which one of the following statements is CORRECT?

   A. Only Sentence I is written in correct English.
   B. Only Sentence II is written in correct English.
   C. Sentences I and II are both written in correct English.
   D. Neither Sentence I nor Sentence II is written in correct English.

14 (#1)

KEY (CORRECT ANSWERS)

1. C
2. A
3. D
4. B
5. C

6. B
7. D
8. A
9. B
10. B

11. C
12. C
13. C
14. B
15. A

16. C
17. B
18. A
19. C
20. A

21. C
22. D
23. A
24. B
25. B

26. A
27. A
28. D
29. D
30. D

31. B
32. C
33. A
34. D
35. A

TEST 2

DIRECTIONS: Each question or incomplete statement is followed by several suggested answers or completions. Select the one that BEST answers the question or completes the statement. *PRINT THE LETTER OF THE CORRECT ANSWER IN THE SPACE AT THE RIGHT.*

Questions 1-5.

DIRECTIONS: Questions 1 through 5 are to be answered SOLELY on the basis of the following information.

Special Officers have the power to arrest members of the public who commit crimes in violation of the Penal Law. Assume that certain classes of crimes covered by various sections of the Penal Law are described below. Special Officers must be able to apply this information when making an arrest in order to accurately determine the type of crime that has been committed.

Crime	Class of Crime	Description of Crime	Section
Petit Larceny	A Misdemeanor	Stealing property worth up to $250	155.25
Grand Larceny 3rd Degree	E Felony	Stealing property worth more than $250	155.30
Grand Larceny 2nd Degree	D Felony	Stealing property worth more than $1,500	155.35
Grand Larceny 1st Degree	C Felony	Stealing property worth any amount of money while making a person fear injury or damage to property	155.40
Assault 3rd Degree	A Misdemeanor	Injuring a person	120.00
Assault 2nd Degree	D Felony	1. Seriously injuring a person; or 2. Injuring an officer of the law	120.05
Assault 1st Degree	C Felony	Seriously injuring a person using a deadly or dangerous weapon	120.10
Disorderly Conduct	Violation	1. Engages in fighting or threatening behavior; or 2. Makes unreasonable noise	240.20
Robbery 3rd Degree	D Felony	Stealing property by force	160.05
Robbery 2nd Degree	C Felony	1. Stealing property by force with the help of another person; or 2. Stealing property by force and injuring any person	160.10
Robbery 1st Degree	B Felony	Stealing property by force and seriously injuring the owner of property	160.15

1. Which one of the following crimes is considered to be Class A Misdemeanor?

   A. Grand Larceny - 3rd Degree
   B. Grand Larceny - 2nd Degree
   C. Assault - 3rd Degree
   D. Assault - 2nd Degree

2. Which one of the following crimes is considered to be Class B Felony?

   A. Robbery - 2nd Degree
   B. Robbery - 1st Degree
   C. Grand Larceny - 3rd Degree
   D. Grand Larceny - 2nd Degree

3. A worker at a facility reports that a typewriter worth $400 has been stolen from her office. Which one of the following is the type of crime that has been committed?

   A. Grand Larceny - 3rd Degree
   B. Grand Larceny - 2nd Degree
   C. Grand Larceny - 1st Degree
   D. Petit Larceny

4. A visitor at a facility begins yelling very loudly at a receptionist and shakes his fist at her. The visitor refuses to stop yelling when an officer tries to calm him down, and he shakes his fist at the officer. Which one of the following is the type of crime that occurred?

   A. Assault - 3rd Degree   B. Assault - 2nd Degree
   C. Assault - 1st Degree   D. Disorderly Conduct

5. An officer has apprehended and arrested a visitor who was attempting to leave the facility with a radio he had stolen from an office. The radio is worth $100.
   Under which one of the following sections of the Penal Law should the visitor be charged? Section

   A. 155.25   B. 155.30   C. 155.35   D. 155.40

Questions 6-12.

DIRECTIONS: Questions 6 through 12 are to be answered SOLELY on the basis of the Arrest Report Form and Incident Report shown on the following page. These reports were submitted by Special Officer John Clark, Shield #512, to his supervisor, Sergeant Joseph Lewis, Shield #818, of the North Bay Health Clinic

Special Officers are required to complete both an Arrest Report Form and an Incident Report whenever an unusual incident or an arrest occurs. The Arrest Report Form provides detailed information regarding the victim and the person arrested, along with a brief description of the incident.

The Incident Report provides a detailed description of the incident. Both reports include the following information: WHO was involved in the incident, including witnesses; WHAT happened and HOW it happened; WHERE and WHEN the incident occurred; and WHY the incident occurred.

ARREST REPORT FORM

ARREST INFORMATION (1)	TIME OF OCCURRENCE 11:15 A.M.	DATE OF OCCURRENCE February 1, 2012	DAY OF WEEK Monday	
INFORMATION ABOUT VICTIM (2)	VICTIM'S NAME Darlene Kirk	ADDRESS 7855 Cruger St., Bronx, NY 10488		
(3)	SEX F	DATE OF BIRTH 9/3/75	RACE White	HOME TELEPHONE # 212-733-3462	SOCIAL SECURITY # 245-63-0772
INFORMATION ABOUT PERSON ARRESTED (4)	NAME OF PERSON ARRESTED Elsie Gardner	ADDRESS 2447 Southern Pkway, Bronx, NY 10467		
(5)	SEX F	DATE OF BIRTH 7/9/80	RACE White	HOME TELEPHONE # 212-513-7029	SOCIAL SECURITY # 244-08-0569
(6)	HEIGHT 5'5"	WEIGHT 135 lbs.	HAIR COLOR Brown	CLOTHING Black coat/red pants	
DESCRIPTION OF CRIME (7)	SECTION OF PENAL LAW 120.00	TYPE OF CRIME Assault - 3rd Degree		
(8)	TIME OF ARREST 11:35 A.M.	DATE OF ARREST 2/1/12	LOCATION OF ARREST 635 Bay Avenue Bronx, NY	
(9)	DESCRIPTION OF INCIDENT The defendant, Elsie Gardner, struck the victim after the victim requested that Ms. Gardner stop smoking in a "NO SMOKING" area. Two witnesses verified the victim's account of the incident.			
INFORMATION ABOUT ARRESTING OFFICER (10)	REPORTING OFFICER'S SIGNATURE *John Clark*	NAME PRINTED John Clark		
(11)	RANK Special Officer	SHIELD NUMBER 512		

INCIDENT REPORT

(1) At 11:15 A.M. on February 1, 2012, I was directed by Sergeant Mark Lewis via two-way radio to report to the Nutrition Clinic on the 4th Floor to investigate a disturbance. (2) Special Officer Anna Colon, Shield #433, was directed to assist me. (3) At 11:16 A.M., Officer Colon and I arrived at the Health Clinic and observed a patient, Elsie Gardner, repeatedly strike Health Clinic receptionist Darlene Kirk about the head and neck. (4) Officer Colon restrained Ms. Gardner while I placed handcuffs on her wrists. (5) Ms. Kirk complained that her neck felt sore. (6) After being examined by Dr. Stone, Ms. Kirk told us that Ms. Gardner entered the Health Clinic at approximately 11:10 A.M. and lit a cigarette in the waiting area. (7) At 11:20 A.M., Dr. Paul Stone examined Ms. Kirk. (8) Ms. Kirk explained to Ms. Gardner that smoking was not allowed in the Health Clinic and showed her the *NO SMOKING* signs posted on the walls. (9) Ms. Gardner ignored Ms. Kirk, and then grew very abusive and attacked her when Ms. Kirk insisted that she stop smoking. (10) Two witnesses, patients Edna Manning of 8937 4th Ave., Bronx, NY, and John Schultz of 357 149th Street, Bronx, NY, gave the same account of the incident as Ms. Kirk. (11) At 11:30 A.M., I read the prisoner her rights and placed her under arrest for violation of Penal Law Section 120.00 -Assault 3rd Degree. (12) At 11:35 A.M., I notified the 86th Precinct of Ms. Gardner's arrest and arranged for the transportation of the prisoner to the precinct. (13) At 11:40 A.M., Officer Colon escorted Ms. Gardner from the Nutrition Clinic to the patrolroom. (14) At 11:55 A.M., Police Officers Cranford, Shield #658, and Wargo, Shield #313, arrived at the facility to transport the prisoner to the precinct. (15) Officer Gray, Shield #936, assumed my post while I reported to the patrolroom to complete the necessary forms concerning the arrest.

6. At what time did Sergeant Lewis inform Officer John Clark of the disturbance in the Nutrition Clinic?
   _____ A.M.

   A. 11:00   B. 11:15   C. 11:16   D. 11:20

7. According to the Arrest Report and the Incident Report, how many witnesses gave the same account of the incident as Ms. Kirk?

   A. 1   B. 2   C. 3   D. 4

8. What information on the Arrest Report is NOT included in the Incident Report?

   A. Date of Occurrence
   B. Victim's address
   C. Section of the Penal Law violated
   D. Assault 3rd Degree

9. Which sentence in the Incident Report is out of order in terms of the sequence of events?

   A. 3   B. 6   C. 11   D. 12

10. According to the Incident Report, at 11:40 A.M. Ms. Gardner was

    A. escorted to the patrolroom
    B. transported to the 86th Precinct
    C. examined by Dr. Paul Stone
    D. giving an account of the incident to Special Officers Clark and Colon

11. According to the Incident Report, which one of the following officers relieved Officer Clark?
    Officer

    A. Colon   B. Cranford   C. Wargo   D. Gray

12. Which section of the Arrest Report contains information that does NOT agree with Sentence 11 of the Incident Report?
    Section

    A. 1   B. 7   C. 8   D. 9

Question 13.

DIRECTIONS: Question 13 is to be answered SOLELY on the basis of the following information.

A Security Officer must investigate any complaint or incident which occurs in the facility, whether he considers it is major or minor. The Officer must also interview the person(s) involved in the incident in order to complete the necessary forms and reports.

5 (#2)

13. Ms. Peters, a clerical worker at the facility, complains to Officer Tynan that a pen set, which had been given to her as a gift, was missing from her desk. She tells Officer Tynan that she knows the pen set was on her desk the previous day because she was using it for her work. Officer Tynan informs Ms. Peters that there is nothing he can do since the pen set was personal property and not facility property.
In this situation, Officer Tynan's response to Ms. Peters is

13._____

A. *correct,* chiefly because the pen set should not have been left out on a desk where it could be stolen
B. *incorrect,* chiefly because a complaint of a loss of theft should be investigated and recorded
C. *correct,* chiefly because Special Officers are only required to investigate a loss or theft of facility property
D. *incorrect,* chiefly because Ms. Peters' work required use of the pen set

Question 14.

DIRECTIONS: Question 14 is to be answered SOLELY on the basis of the following information.

Assume that Security Officers are responsible for recording in a personal memobook all of their routine and non-routine activities and occurrences for each tour of duty. Before starting a tour of duty, a Security Officer must enter in his personal memobook the date, tour, and assigned post. An entry shall be made to record each absence from duty, such as a regular day off, sick leave, annual leave, or holiday. During each tour, a Security Officer shall enter a full and accurate record of duties performed, changes in post assignment, absences from post, and the reason for each absence, and all other patrol business.

14. Security Officer Ella Lewis is assigned to Gotham Center Facility, where she works Monday through Friday on a 9:00 A.M. to 5:00 P.M. tour. Officer Lewis' regular days off are Saturday and Sunday. Officer Lewis worked on Wednesday, November 25, 2012. She was absent on Thursday, November 26, 2012, for Thanksgiving Holiday, and on Friday, November 27, 2012, for annual leave.
According to the information given above, which of the following entries is the FIRST entry that Officer Lewis should record in her memobook when she returns to work on November 30, 2012?

14._____

A. Saturday, 11/28/12 and Sunday, 11/29/12 - Regular days off
B. Friday, 11/27/12 - Sick Leave
C. Monday, 11/30/12 - On duty
D. Thursday, 11/26/12 - Thanksgiving Holiday

Questions 15-16.

DIRECTIONS: Questions 15 and 16 are to be answered SOLELY on the basis of the following entries recorded by Security Officer Angela Russo in her memobook.

Date: January 8, 2012
Tour: 8:00 A.M. to 4:00 P.M.
Weather: Sunny and clear

111

6 (#2)

7:30   Reported to B Command for Roll Call. Assigned to Post #2,
C Building Emergency Room Corridor by Sergeant Robert Floyd.
Break: 9:30 A.M.
Meal: 1:30 P.M.
Radio: #701

7:40   Arrived at Post #2 and relieved Special Officer Johnson, Shield #593.

7:45   On patrol - Post #2.

8:00   Post #2 - All secure at this time; conditions normal.

8:30   Fire Alarm Box 5-3-1 rings on 3rd Floor South in C Building.
Upon arrival, Office Worker Molly Lewis reported that a waste-paper basket was on fire. Used fire extinguisher to put out fire.

8:50   Condition corrected; Incident Report prepared and submitted to Sergeant Floyd in B Command.

8:55   Resumed patrol of Post #2.

9:30   Relieved for break by Officer Tucker.

9:50   Resumed patrol of Post #2.

10:10   Disorderly person reported by Clinic Director Lila Jones on Ward C-32; Officer Bailey and myself responded. Clinic Director Jones informed officers that visitor Bradley Manna, male white, 19 years of age, 2 Park Place, Brooklyn, NY, is drunk and has been shouting insults to Clinic staff.

10:30   Condition corrected; Visitor Bradley Manna escorted off premises. B Command notified of incident.

10:40   Resumed patrol of Post #2.

11:40   Post #2 - All secure at this time.

12:40   Post #2 - All secure at this time.

15. The name of the Clinic Director who reported a disorderly person is   15.____

    A. Molly Lewis   B. Bradley Manna
    C. Lila Jones   D. Robert Floyd

16. Which of the following sets of officers responded to the report of a disorderly person on   16.____
Ward C-32?
Officers

    A. Johnson and Bailey   B. Russo and Tucker
    C. Johnson and Tucker   D. Russo and Bailey

17. Security Officer Mace is completing an entry in her memo-book. The entry has the following five sentences:
    1. I observed the defendant removing a radio from a facility vehicle.
    2. I placed the defendant under arrest and escorted him to the patrolroom.
    3. I was patrolling the facility parking lot.
    4. I asked the defendant to show identification.
    5. I determined that the defendant was not authorized to remove the radio.

    The MOST logical order for these sentences to be entered in Officer Mace's memo-book is

    A. 1, 3, 2, 4, 5
    B. 2, 5, 4, 1, 3
    C. 3, 1, 4, 5, 2
    D. 4, 5, 2, 1, 3

18. Security Officer Riley is completing an entry in his memo-book. The entry has the following five sentences:
    1. Anna Jones admitted that she stole Mary Green's wallet.
    2. I approached the women and asked them who they were and why they were arguing.
    3. I arrested Anna Jones for stealing Mary Green's wallet.
    4. They identified themselves and Mary Green accused Anna Jones of stealing her wallet.
    5. I was in the lobby area when I observed two women arguing about a wallet.

    The MOST logical order for these sentences to be entered in Officer Riley's memobook is

    A. 2, 4, 1, 3, 5
    B. 3, 1, 4, 5, 2
    C. 4, 1, 5, 2, 3
    D. 5, 2, 4, 1, 3

19. Assume that Security Officer John Ryan is completing an entry in his memobook. The entry has the following five sentences:
    1. I then cleared the immediate area of visitors and staff.
    2. I noticed smoke coming from a broom closet outside Room A71.
    3. Sergeant Mueller arrived with other officers to assist in clearing the area.
    4. Upon investigation, I determined the smoke was due to burning material in the broom closet.
    5. I pulled the corridor fire alarm and notified Sergeant Mueller of the fire.

    The MOST logical order for these sentences to be entered in Officer Ryan's memo-book is

    A. 2, 3, 4, 5, 1
    B. 2, 4, 5, 1, 3
    C. 4, 1, 2, 3, 5
    D. 5, 3, 2, 1, 4

20. Security Officer Hernandez is completing an entry in his memobook. The entry has the following five sentences:
    1. I asked him to leave the premises immediately.
    2. A visitor complained that there was a strange man loitering in Clinic B hallway.
    3. I went to investigate and saw a man dressed in rags sitting on the floor of the hallway.
    4. As he walked out, he started yelling that he had no place to go.
    5. I asked to see identification, but he said that he did not have any.

    The MOST logical order for these sentences to be entered in Officer Hernandez's memobook is

A.	2, 3, 5, 1, 4	B.	3, 1, 2, 4, 5
C.	4, 1, 5, 2, 3	D.	3, 1, 5, 2, 4

21. Officer Hogan is completing an entry in his memobook. The entry has the following five sentences:
    1. When the fighting had stopped, I transmitted a message requesting medical assistance for Mr. Perkins.
    2. Special Officer Manning assisted me in stopping the fight.
    3. When I arrived at the scene, I saw a client, Adam Finley strike a facility employee, Peter Perkins.
    4. As I attempted to break up the fight, Special Officer Manning came on the scene.
    5. I received a radio message from Sergeant Valez to investigate a possible fight in progress in the waiting room.

    The MOST logical order for these sentences to be entered in Officer Hogan's memobook is

A.	2, 1, 4, 5, 3	B.	3, 5, 2, 4, 1
C.	4, 5, 3, 1, 2	D.	5, 3, 4, 2, 1

Questions 22-23.

DIRECTIONS: Questions 22 and 23 are to be answered SOLELY on the basis of the following information.

Assume that Security Officers may be assigned to the facility patrolroom and must follow the guidelines below in documenting all routine and non-routine activities and occurrences in the facility logbook.

At the beginning of each tour of duty, the Security Officer responsible for entering information in the logbook must transfer from the Roll Call Sheet to the logbook a list of all security staff personnel assigned to that tour. This list is to be entered in order of the rank of the security staff member. All other entries in the facility logbook shall be recorded in chronological order, in blue or black ink, and be neat and legible.

22. When recording the list of security staff personnel assigned to a tour, that entry shall be made in

    A. chronological order
    B. order of rank of security staff
    C. alphabetical order
    D. order of arrival at facility

23. A Security Officer has transmitted notification to the patrolroom that he has just issued a summons. The Security Officer responsible for documenting occurrences in the patrolroom logbook should record the information

    A. in red ink, immediately following the previous entry
    B. on a new page under the heading *Summonses Reported*
    C. in blue or black ink immediately following the previous entry
    D. on the last page of the logbook where it can be easily found

Question 24.

DIRECTIONS: Question 24 is to be answered SOLELY on the basis of the following information.

Assume that whenever a Security Officer is to begin a leave of absence, long-term sick leave, or other type of leave having an anticipated length of ten days or more, the officer shall surrender his or her security shield to his supervisor, who shall immediately forward it to Security Headquarters.

24. Two male clients were fighting in the waiting room of North End Hospital. Officer Gary Klott attempted to separate them and became involved in the altercation. Officer Klott sustained an injury to the right eye and was examined by a physician. The physician directed Officer Klott to stay home for a recovery period of 12 days. In this situation, Officer Klott should

    A. surrender his shield to his supervisor
    B. safeguard his shield in a safe place at home while he is recovering
    C. surrender his shield to the physician
    D. safeguard his shield with his uniform in his locker at the facility while he is recovering

24._____

Question 25.

DIRECTIONS: Question 25 is to be answered SOLELY on the basis of the following information.

Assume that Security Officers are required to follow certain procedures when on post at a restricted area of a facility. They must inspect the identification of employees and passes of visitors, as well as all bags and packages carried by individuals who wish to enter the restricted area.

25. Security Officer Stevens is assigned to a post at the Intensive Care Unit of Park View Hospital, a restricted area. Officer Stevens is responsible for inspecting identification and passes, as well as all bags and packages carried by individuals who want to enter the Unit. He sees Mr. Craig approach. He knows Mr. Craig's wife is a patient in the Unit. Officer Stevens has seen Mr. Craig visit his wife every day for the past four days. Mr. Craig brings a small duffel bag filled with magazines each time he comes. Today, Officer Stevens checks Mr. Craig's visitor's pass but lets Mr. Craig enter the Unit without checking his duffel bag. In this situation, Officer Stevens' action is

    A. *correct*, chiefly because he has checked to see that Mr. Craig has a visitor's pass
    B. *incorrect*, chiefly because all packages and bags must be inspected before anyone is allowed to enter a restricted area
    C. *correct*, chiefly because he is familiar with Mr. Craig and knows that he only carries magazines in his duffel bag
    D. *incorrect*, chiefly because Mr. Craig should not be allowed to carry a bag or package into a restricted area of the facility

25._____

Question 26.

DIRECTIONS: Question 26 is to be answered SOLELY on the basis of the following information.

Assume that Special Officers must safeguard evidence in cases involving firearms. Special Officers must mark recovered bullets for identification purposes. The Officer who recovers the bullet must mark his or her initials and the date of recovery of the bullet on the base or on the nose of the bullet.

26. On January 18, 2012, at 11:30 P.M., an unidentified person fired a shot at an unoccupied security patrol car in the facility parking lot. Officer Debra Johnson was assigned to investigate the matter. A fired bullet was recovered inside the patrol car by Officer Johnson at 1:00 A.M. on January 19, 2012.
Officer Johnson should mark *D.J. 1/19/12* on

   A. the base or the nose of the recovered bullet
   B. the side of the recovered bullet
   C. an envelope and place the recovered bullet inside
   D. the side of the patrol car from which the bullet was recovered

Question 27.

DIRECTIONS: Question 27 is to be answered SOLELY on the basis of the following information.

Patrolroom Observers are officers who are assigned to observe events when individuals, other than security staff, are present in the patrolroom. According to facility guidelines, a Patrolroom Observer must be called to the patrolroom to serve as a witness whenever any individual is brought to the patrolroom for any reason by a Special Officer.

27. Janet Childs, a client at Gotham Health Facility, was robbed in the facility's parking lot. Ms. Childs was not harmed as a result of the incident, but she was upset. Special Officer Grey escorted her to the patrol-room, where she remained until she felt better. While she was waiting in the patrolroom, Officer Grey did not call a Patrolman Observer to the patrolroom during the time that Ms. Childs was there.
In this situation, Officer Grey

   A. should not have taken Ms. Childs to the patrolroom without special authorization from his supervisor
   B. was not required to call a Patrolroom Observer to the patrolroom since Ms. Childs had not been placed under arrest
   C. should have called a Patrolroom Observer to be present while Ms. Childs was in the patrolroom
   D. should have escorted Ms. Childs to the patrolroom and left her in the care of the Special Officer assigned to the patrolroom

Question 28.

DIRECTIONS: Question 28 is to be answered SOLELY on the basis of the following information.

Special Officers escort individuals categorized as Emotionally Disturbed Persons to the hospital for observation or treatment when directed to do so. These individuals are transported to the hospital by Emergency Medical Service (EMS) ambulance. There must be one Special Officer present in the ambulance for each Emotionally Disturbed Person transferred to the hospital, along with an EMS Technician and the ambulance driver.

28. Special Officers Patrick Lawson and Grace Martin have been assigned to escort two individuals categorized as Emotionally Disturbed Persons from that facility to a nearby hospital. The EMS ambulance, with an EMS Technician and ambulance driver, has arrived at the facility to transport the individuals. Officer Lawson then suggests to Officer Martin that it is not necessary for him to go to the hospital since the EMS Technician will be with Officer Martin in the ambulance.
In this situation, Officer Lawson's suggestion is 28.____

    A. *correct*, since an EMS Technician will be present in the ambulance to accompany Officer Martin and the Emotionally Disturbed Persons to the hospital
    B. *incorrect*, since one Special Officer must be present in the ambulance for each Emotionally Disturbed Person transported to the hospital
    C. *correct*, since the Emotionally Disturbed Persons are unlikely to cause any disturbance inside the ambulance
    D. *incorrect*, since two EMS Technicians must be present in the ambulance when only one Special Officer is escorting two Emotionally Disturbed Persons to the hospital

Questions 29-32.

DIRECTIONS: Questions 29 through 32 are to be answered on the basis of the following information.

Assume that information concerning new or updated policies and procedures are sometimes provided to facility security staff in the form of a memorandum from Security Headquarters.

Question 29.

DIRECTIONS: Question 29 is to be answered SOLELY on the basis of the following memorandum.

TO: All Security Officers
FROM: Security Headquarters
SUBJECT: Smoking Regulations

At times, Security Officers have been observed smoking while on duty at their assigned posts. This is strictly prohibited. If Officers feel that they must smoke, they may smoke during breaks or lunch period in designated areas. Officers may not smoke while on official duty. If any Officer is observed smoking while on post or while performing official duties, appropriate disciplinary action will be taken.

29. According to the above memorandum, Security Officers may

   A. smoke while on duty, as long as they are out of view of the public
   B. not smoke while on duty except when assigned to a post in a designated smoking area
   C. smoke on breaks or during lunch period in designated areas
   D. not smoke at any time when dressed in official uniform

Question 30.

DIRECTIONS: Question 30 is to be answered SOLELY on the basis of the following memorandum.

TO: All Special Officers
FROM: Security Headquarters
SUBJECT: Safeguarding Shields and Identification Cards

Special Officers must ensure that their shields and identification cards are secure at all times. Should an officer become aware of the loss or theft of his shield or identification card, he shall immediately report such loss or theft to Security Headquarters.

30. According to the above memorandum, a Special Officer must

   A. report the loss or theft of his identification card to the nearest police precinct
   B. secure his shield in his locker at all times
   C. report the loss or theft of his shield or identification card to Security Headquarters immediately
   D. secure his identification card at Security Headquarters each night before leaving the facility

Question 31.

DIRECTIONS: Question 31 is to be answered SOLELY on the basis of the following memorandum.

TO: All Security Officers
FROM: Security Headquarters
SUBJECT: Fire in the Facility

Special Officers must report immediately to assist at the scene of a fire when directed to do so by a supervisor. Officers shall remain at the scene and ensure that only authorized personnel are in an area restricted by a fire emergency. Visitors and clients shall be directed to the nearest safe stairwell and out of the facility. Visitors and clients are not to use elevators to evacuate the area.

31. According to the above memorandum, a Security Officer should

   A. direct visitors and clients to the nearest elevator in case of fire
   B. report unauthorized personnel at a fire scene to the Fire Department
   C. escort visitors and clients down the nearest stairwell and out of the facility
   D. ensure that only authorized personnel are in an area restricted by a fire emergency

Question 32.

DIRECTIONS: Question 32 is to be answered SOLELY on the basis of the following memorandum.

TO: All Security Officers
FROM: Security Headquarters
SUBJECT: Reporting Unsafe Conditions

Security Officers shall report to their supervisors and appropriate facility staff any condition that could affect the safety or security of the facility. Conditions such as broken windows, unlocked doors and water leaks should be reported.

32. According to the above memorandum, a Security Officer shall

   A. make recommendations to his superiors concerning other facility staff members
   B. correct all unsafe conditions such as broken windows
   C. report a condition such as a water leak to his supervisor and appropriate facility staff
   D. make recommendations to facility staff concerning doors to be left unlocked

33. Following are two sentences that may or may not be written in correct English:
   I. Special Officer Cleveland was attempting to calm an emotionally disturbed visitor.
   II. The visitor did not stops crying and calling for his wife.
   Which one of the following statements is CORRECT?

   A. Only Sentence I is written in correct English.
   B. Only Sentence II is written in correct English.
   C. Sentences I and II are both written in correct English.
   D. Neither Sentence I nor Sentence II is written in correct English.

34. Following are two sentences that may or may not be written in correct English:
   I. While on patrol, I observes a vagrant loitering near the drug dispensary.
   II. I escorted the vagrant out of the building and off the premises.
   Which one of the following statements is CORRECT?

   A. Only Sentence I is written in correct English.
   B. Only Sentence II is written in correct English.
   C. Sentences I and II are both written in correct English.
   D. Neither Sentence I nor Sentence II is written in correct English.

35. Following are two sentences that may or may not be written in correct English:
   I. At 4:00 P.M., Sergeant Raymond told me to evacuate the waiting area immediately due to a bomb threat.
   II. Some of the clients did not want to leave the building.
   Which one of the following statements is CORRECT?

   A. Only Sentence I is written in correct English.
   B. Only Sentence II is written in correct English.
   C. Sentences I and II are both written in correct English.
   D. Neither Sentence I nor Sentence II is written in correct English.

KEY (CORRECT ANSWERS)

1.	C	16.	D
2.	B	17.	C
3.	A	18.	D
4.	D	19.	B
5.	A	20.	A
6.	B	21.	D
7.	B	22.	B
8.	B	23.	C
9.	B	24.	A
10.	A	25.	B
11.	D	26.	A
12.	C	27.	C
13.	B	28.	B
14.	D	29.	C
15.	C	30.	C

31.	D
32.	C
33.	A
34.	B
35.	C

POLICE SCIENCE NOTES
FIREARMS – CARE, MAINTENANCE, AND FAMILIARIZATION

IMPORTANCE OF POLICE FIREARMS

The police are the action group called upon to enforce the regulations of the lawfully constituted government of the community. Unfortunately, laws are sometimes actively resisted, occasionally with deadly force. Such life-endangering incidents require the police to overcome the resistance with equal or superior force, the ultimate being through use of firearms.

Most officers go through their entire careers without the necessity of firing their weapons at a person, and some without ever being required to even draw their weapons. Daily, however, other police officers somewhere are faced with the dire necessity to protect themselves or others by the use of their firearms. One is reminded of the rhyme from the early days of the repeating handgun:

> Be not afraid of any man
> > no matter what his size.
> When danger threatens call on me,
> > and I will equalize.

But no officer should suffer under the mistaken belief that he becomes "equal" simply because he carries a firearm. Rather, he must be well trained and practiced in order to accomplish these two important objectives:

1. The professional police officer must know the circumstances under which the use of his firearm is *essential* so that he will utilize its deadly force *only* under such conditions.

2. The professional police officer must, through practice, become proficient in the use of firearms so that he will be superior to those few opponents who attack with deadly force.

Police professionals look forward to the time when advanced weapons are available which will instantly incapacitate attackers without deadly force, and such are being presently developed. However, until then officers must utilize firearms which kill when immediate incapacitation of an aggressor is essential to protect life.

Proficiency in the use of firearms can be developed only through periodic practice performed at least monthly if at all possible. There are essentially two types of shooting practice utilized by police. The first is shooting at stationary bullseye targets, which requires considerable accuracy as the target is small. Shooting at this type of target with a handgun is performed entirely by operating the weapon single action. The second type of practice is that of combat or "practical" courses in which the targets are human silhouettes and/or moving or disappearing. When this type of course is performed with a handgun, it is ordinarily fired double action.

Each officer should avail himself of every opportunity to increase his skill with the firearms utilized by his department, even if it is only by dry firing. Combat situations arise unexpectedly, and there is little time to think. Unless the proper habits and skills have been well developed by constant practice, the officer may fail in his attempt to protect his own life or that of another. There may be opportunity for only one shot before it is too late; it must be a good one.

It is not possible here to provide a detailed explanation of how to shoot well or to provide comprehensive instruction in firearms. That must be learned from expert instructors and perfected through practice. It is hoped, however, that each officer will come to know his weapons, use them accurately, and fire them only under appropriate and lawful circumstances. Those are the marks of the professional officer.

POLICE FIREARMS

At present, police firearms are all small arms and include handguns (also termed "sidearms"), shotguns (also called "riot guns" when equipped—as they usually are—with barrel shorter than those used for hunting purposes), tear gas guns, automatic weapons, and rifles. Hand and tear gas guns can be thought of as "defensive" weapons, although some handguns are now available which fire bullets at velocity; formerly possible only with shoulder weapons. The remaining firearms are "offensive" weapons fired from the shoulder. An offensive weapon is one which would be utilized against an extremely dangerous and well-armed aggressor because of its larger caliber, higher muzzle velocity, longer range, greater accuracy or rapid rate of fire. Offensive weapons are used when it is necessary to attack and kill.

The following are some of the terms used to identify or describe police firearms:

Small Arm: Firearm capable of being fired while hand held or held with the hands and braced against the shoulder.

Shoulder Weapon: Firearm normally fired while held with the hands and braced against the shoulder.

Rifle: Shoulder weapon with a rifled bore.

Shotgun: Smooth bore shoulder weapon; generally loaded with shot shells but rifled slugs are also used.

Handgun/Sidearm: Firearm normally held, aimed, and fired with one hand.

Pistol: Handgun with integral chamber and barrel.

Revolver: Handgun with a cylinder containing several chambers which are moved successively into line with the barrel to be fired.

Automatic/Machine Pistol/Submachine Gun/Machine Gun: Self-loading firearm capable of continuous fire as long as the trigger remains pulled.

Semi-Automatic/Autoloader: Self-loading firearm which will fire only one shot each time the trigger is pulled and not another until it is first released.

NOTE: When a weapon is called a machine gun, machine pistol, or submachine gun, it will always be a truly automatic firearm capable of continuous fire until the trigger is released. However, the terms "automatic pistol" or "automatic shotgun" are commonly used in referring to weapons which are actually semi-automatics (autoloaders). A true "automatic rifle" is a machine gun, but the term is popularly used for semi-automatic rifles also. A rare handgun is the automatic revolver; few have been manufactured, and the police do not use them.

The energy utilized for the self-loading operation of an automatic or autoloader weapon is that of the previously fired round's recoil or its gas pressure acting upon a piston. Therefore, auto weapons are referred to as being either recoil or gas operated.

Caliber: The measurement in decimal (expressed in hundredths, i.e., .22, .32, etc., or thousandths, i.e., .223, .300, .357, etc.) parts of an inch of a firearms bore diameter between opposite lands.

Gauge: The size of a shotguns bore expressed by the number of lead spheres, each precisely fitting that bore, which would weigh one pound.

Groove/Rifling: The spiral channels (usually numbering from four to six) which have been cut into the bore to impart rotation to the bullet during its passage. The gyroscopic action of the spinning bullet prevents its tumbling during flight and increases accuracy.

Lands: The surface of the bore between adjacent grooves.

Single Action: Cocking a handgun manually before each shot, or a handgun which must be manually cocked (for the first shot if it is an autoloader).

Double Action: A firearm designed so that operating the trigger cocks the weapon (for the first shot if it is an autoloader), or the firing of a weapon by employing its double action capability.

Dry Firing: Practicing with an unloaded weapon; sighting; squeezing the trigger, cocking, etc.

CARE OF FIREARMS

The critical factor for the proper maintenance of police firearms is simply that of firing them under a planned, periodic schedule. Not only does such use prove each weapon's ability to function properly (or not), but the officers become more proficient through the practice involved.

Quality firearms which are well maintained last for more than a lifetime, and the wear caused by firing them is usually the least important factor in causing malfunctions. If a police firearm fails to shoot as it should, the cause is most likely to be negligence in its care by the officer to whom it has been issued. Maintenance is simple. The officer need only keep a *light* coating of oil on exposed and moving parts and run a swab through the barrel and cylinders weekly and perform these easy tasks immediately after the gun's exposure to unusual dampness or dirt. In short, it should simply be kept clean and rust free.

Faulty ammunition is the next most likely cause for malfunction. Cartridges more than a year old should not be carried on duty. Excessive oiling of the weapon at any point where that oil can contact and seep into the rounds must be avoided to prevent cartridge malfunction. Although rounds should be kept free of dirt, moisture, and corrosion, they should be neither oiled nor polished, merely wiped clean with a dry rag.

Inability to fire or inaccuracy can be caused by accidental damage inflicted by dropping a weapon or other impacts received by it. Such blows can bend or break parts of the weapon or damage and misalign the sights. Immediately after a firearm is dropped, struck, or otherwise receives an impact, it should be carefully examined for damage. Any problem should be corrected immediately. Unless it is obvious that the repair required is minimal and within the capability of the person performing it, the weapon should be sent to a gunsmith.

Another common cause of malfunction is that of work performed for repair or to "improve" a weapon by a person who is insufficiently skilled in the craft of the gunsmith. Too often trigger pulls are lightened or spring tensions changed, to improve accuracy on the target range, to the point at which the gun becomes extremely dangerous to handle or fails to fire at all. Firearms are finely machined devices which can be ruined by the inexperienced.

SAFETY RULES

A gun is a machine designed to kill and it will do so whether or not the person possessing it intends such a result when he fires the weapon or permits its accidental discharge. There is an old saying among experienced police officers that, "More policemen are shot by policemen than by criminals." Following the suggestions below will prevent most accidental deaths and injuries caused by firearms.

No person should fire a weapon unless and until he is aware of where the bullet may strike. This includes the target at which he is aiming *and* any other person or thing likely to be hit if he misses or the bullet passes through the target.

Every gun should be assumed as being loaded by every person who has not had the opportunity to personally inspect it.

Whenever possible, if a firearm is to be passed to another, it should be either unloaded or the action opened (or the cylinder of a revolver swung out). If it is loaded when passed, however, the statement, "This is loaded," should be expressed *and* acknowledged.

Guns should be kept away from children and the inexperienced either by being locked away or immobilized with a locking device on the weapons themselves. Various types of gun locks are available and a revolver can be "locked" by swinging the cylinder out and locking handcuffs through the frame in its place.

Firing or fingering the trigger while on the run is extremely hazardous and to be consciously avoided even during combat.

A gun should *never* be pointed at a person unless firing it would be necessary and lawful under the conditions existing or imminently expected to arise.

Holding a person at bay with a cocked double-action firearm is extremely hazardous because of the great possibility of accidental discharge, and is to be consciously avoided.

ON THE FIRING RANGE

The gun should not be loaded until time for firing or, if there is a range master, by command.

A loaded weapon should never be pointed in any direction except downrange toward the target.

No shooter should turn to leave his firing position unless his weapon is first unloaded and its action opened or the gun holstered.

A shooter should not continue to shoot after a misfire or short round (insufficient or no powder).

NOTE: The gun should remain pointed downrange with its action closed for one or two minutes in case the misfire goes off late. After a short round, the barrel must be inspected to make certain that the bullet has cleared it.

Each shooter should remain alert for those who disregard safety and range regulations. Such negligent persons should be either personally requested to mend their ways or reported to the range master.

DECISIONS COMMONLY MADE BY AGENCIES ON FIREARMS

Executives of police departments are faced with the need to study their agency's firearm requirements and to make appropriate decisions concerning the weapons which their officers will be required or permitted to utilize. Following are some of the matters which must be determined:

Sidearm: Specified make or model, revolver or autoloader, barrel length, target grips or standard (some target grips interfere with reloading or shooting with either hand), type of finish, caliber, single or double action, sensitivity of trigger pull, type of sights, and "back-up" or second gun.

Ammunition: Magnum or standard, specified brand(s), weight of bullet, special reloads or factory only, bullet configuration (round, semiwadcutter, hollowpoint, shot packet, jacketed, etc.), age, size of shot and/or rifled slug for shotguns, number of extra rounds or clips to be carried, and type of holder in which additional ammunition is carried.

Sidearm Holsters: Belt, swivel, cross-draw, shoulder, spring, full cover, hammer strap, concealed, and spring-opening.

Shoulder Weapons: Shotgun, rifle, gauge or caliber, barrel length, hand or auto-load, full automatic, type of sights, carried in passenger compartment or trunk, readily visible or concealed, secured by locking device or simple holder only, equipped with breakable seal, carried with chambered round or not, and supplied to each patrol car or only carried by supervisors or retained at headquarters.

The critical decision is always that which determines whether or not human life will be taken or placed in grave peril. It is hoped that every officer faced with such a decision will act morally and lawfully because of his professional training and experience.

POLICE SCIENCE NOTES

BASIC CONCEPTS OF LAW AND ARREST

Man has been puzzling over the appropriateness of community controls throughout his recorded history and undoubtedly before that. What he has been trying to decide are the answers to: "Who is/are going to run the show?" "Under what restrictions must authority operate?" and "What acts by community members shall be required or prohibited?" Basic to an understanding of the complexity of answers to these questions is an awareness of the variety of systems and laws under which various societies have lived and are living. At some time some community has lived under laws directly opposite to those under which we now control ourselves, and their requirements were "right" for that time and place. In fact, we can bring to mind examples of changes which have occurred in our own United States of America during its existence—even within our own lifetime. The requirements placed upon the members of any community by its government consist of laws which filter out by prevailing over others in the market place of ideas and which are manifested by their issuance through formal governmental organizations.

Every police office should be aware of the fact that there is no law which has not been enacted in response to and for the purpose of correcting a problem which has become significant by the degree to which some member of the community have acted in opposition to the common belief. In short, where there is no meaningful opposition to the feelings of the majority there is no law in support of those beliefs. For example, cannibalism is not prohibited in the United States because opposition to it is so pervasive that it is reasonable to say that only the mentally ill have engaged in that gruesome activity.

Individuals and communities require guidelines defining acceptable conduct and reciprocal duties and responsibilities in order to attain feelings of tranquility, a sense of well-being, and a belief that conformance to group requirements will result in the society's respect for and supply of individual needs in response. Basic to any society, primitive or modern, is the necessity for disciplined behavior, and the necessity for community tranquility. Each individual must relinquish his right to act entirely for his own self-interest in return for the agreement of others not to deprive him unduly of his right to personal freedom or to impinge upon his reciprocal rights under the law. Every requirement of law acts to some degree to reduce individual freedom of action, but reasonable restrictions on absolute freedom are essential to community living and to protect individuals against others. As the danger to any community belief increases so will the group response grow in severity to reduce that threat, especially when the common belief is basic and widely accepted without reservation.

Police officers are faced with daily frustration caused by their inability to understand clearly that the freedom-loving citizens of our Nation have learned from past experience (some of which initiated our Nation's birth) that absolute authority demands rigid compliance with even the smallest and relatively unimportant requirement and results in stultifying repression of personal freedom. The ultimately efficient government can only be one in which power is so centralized that it is dictatorial and undemocratic. Therefore, laws have developed which restrict the police to that level of efficiency which is acceptable to the citizens and which permits the greatest possible individual freedom. Again, there is no law where there is no problem. Therefore, there should be little serious doubt that one of the highest duties of a police officer is to know and follow the law because it has been developed in answer to previously existing actions which were conducted in opposition to the beliefs of the people. Officials who are responsible for law enforcement must personify lawfulness as they interact with offenders. A peace officer is endowed with awesome power over life and property, and he must not only restrict his actions to those the law but also restrain himself personally to be considered a thoughtful, objective, police professional.

It is important that every police officer understands the basics of the checks and balances system under which we govern ourselves. Our forefathers so constructed our governmental system that none of the three branches of our government—the legislature, the executive, and the judicial—could become so strong that it would be able to dominate the people completely. The basic objective of this system is to prevent one or a few people from absolute control and overwhelming power. In its operation, the checks and balances system prevents domination by providing stumbling blocks in the paths of requirements which do not meet with the approval of the great majority of the citizens. Without considerable support, legislatures will not pass laws, the executive branch will not actively enforce them, and the courts will overturn them. However, those requirements which are backed by the great majority of the people are enacted by legislatures, enforced with great universality and vigor by the executive branch, and upheld by the courts.

The individual professional police officer understands the checks and balances system and acts within the law because of this knowledge. At the operational level, even though a patrol officer is aware of a problem he does not attempt to "enforce the law" when the legislature has not passed a statute dealing with it. He neither strains to fit the facts of an incident into another statute nor makes an arrest for an unrelated offense in order to harrass the "law breaker." At the executive level, the professional police administrator or agency head allocates the resources of his department according to priorities so that enforcement of important offenses is emphasized. The accompanying spinoff is naturally the de-emphasis of enforcement against those offenses which are determined to be of lesser importance. The term which applies to this assignment of priorities is *selective enforcement*.

Professional Demeanor

The appropriateness of the reasons for and the manner by which members of a community are deprived of their liberty is one of the most difficult problems to be solved by members of a society and its lawmakers. An arrest or detention is a matter of preventing the free movement of a person. In most cases, what is more important to the person subject to this deprivation of liberty is the manner in which an arrest or detention is effected. There is a great difference between simply following the directions of another without the free will to do any other thing one might wish to do and that loss *plus* being searched, handcuffed, placed in obvious incarceration, and even being stripped of all clothing and dignity for the purpose of maximizing security. In fact, most people will understand the necessity of appropriate loss of liberty, but what makes them seriously upset is the public spectacle and loss of face which it can entail when improperly conducted, especially when the arresting officer shows personal antagonism toward the prisoner.

The professional officer balances the importance of each factor involved in an arrest situation. Although safety to himself, his fellow officers and the general public is very important, he is well aware that it is not always the most important factor. In fact, he knows that some persons will submit to an arrest quietly unless demeaning security precautions are utilized or personal antagonism is manifested by the arresting officer. Unfortunately, the unprofessional officer often considers security and safety to be uppermost and controlling in nearly every case and is personally offended by lawbreakers. When these conditions prevail, arrested and detained persons are often subjected to such overwhelming threats to their psychological well-being (or face) that they find it necessary to fight back against those who are creating the threat. in some cases their loss of face or distress is so great that they physically attack any person who obstructs their liberty and are willing to kill to escape rather than to suffer the public humiliation of detention or arrest. Therefore, the professional officer effects his detentions and arrests with circumspection and avoids excessive psychological distress to those being restricted. By making the arrest as easy as possible on the offender, the arresting officer also makes it as easy as possible on himself and his coworkers. The professional exerts his will over those whom he is arresting by the use of reasoning rather than his club. The officer who is involved in fights significantly more often than his coworkers, however soon becomes well known and is avoided as a partner.

Persons usually react in three general ways to a police officer who is enforcing the law or is about to make an arrest. They may submit to his directions or the arrest without resistance. Such persons follow the directions of the officer because they believe that the officer is correct in what he is doing or they simply bow to the inevitable. The professional, skilled police officer will so conduct himself that the great majority of persons will react to his directions in this way.

Other persons may feel gravely threatened by the officer's actions and believe it necessary to attack either verbally or physically, or flee. Whatever their action may be, it is an attempt to reduce the real or imagined threat to their physical or mental well-being. Although the attack will usually be directed at the source of the threat, the officer, it may be against another person—an "innocent" third party. This is still an attempt to reduce their feelings of frustration, however, but the target will be an object or person who cannot "fight back." We have all witnessed examples of distressed persons who kick their cats, shout at their children, or drive their automobiles recklessly when frustrated. In fact, many times officers find themselves to be the "cat" whom it is necessary for the person to "kick" to compensate for a frustrating experience which occurred prior to the officer's arrival on the scene. The professional officer, because of his self-confidence, is never threatened by verbal "cat kicking." He is able to control these excited persons through the use of his calm, professional, competent manner so that they soon begin to accept his directions. This same technique is usually effective with those offenders who are inclined towards physical attack. The experienced professional officer knows with reasonable accuracy those who cannot be dissuaded and with reasonable force acts to protect himself and others from physical attack.

The professional officer asks himself questions such as these: "This person is attacking me verbally, therefore, he (NOT I) is greatly threatened by something. Am I the threat, or is it something else?" "Is this attack going to be all talk, or will it turn into a physical attack?" "What can I do to reduce his feeling of distress?" The unprofessional reacts out of his own fear of the verbal attack, retaliates in kind, and the situation rapidly escalates into physical combat or the bringing of inappropriate charges out of spite. Invariably the result of retaliatory action by an officer who attacks to save his own face, no matter how poorly the offender may have acted to initiate the incident, is the salvation of the offender's conscience. This is because the offender will be able to say to himself that the officer attacked him, therefore, no matter what the offender has done, the officer has become the "bad guy" who is subject to all the blame—the "offensive cat," if you will

The third reaction is that of ignoring or remaining unaffected by the threat. Persons who manifest this type of reaction are those who are secure, unconcerned, and believe that they are truly not endangered by the threat. They are convinced that those who are acting aggressively towards them cannot in fact harm them in any basic way. In everyday language, this type of individual is called a person with "self-confidence." It is this type of confidence that the professional police officer exhibits. It is a quiet confidence, as opposed to the blatant, pushy, aggressive, officious manner of those who are unsure of themselves and who try to make up for it with bluster, which is immediately recognizable as a lack of confidence.

Self-confidence is the kind of attitude which makes it possible to exert one's will upon others while encountering the least resistance from them. The officer who exhibits this confidence brings the belief into the minds of those he is controlling that: "This officer will not ask anything of me which is not only lawful but also reasonable and necessary, and if I refuse to act in response to his requests, I will be not only lawful but also unreasonable and appear foolish to others." On the other hand, if it is the person who is to be arrested who exhibits the self-confidence, that person is the one who has the greatest chance of defeating the officer and taking over control of the situation. The officer who allows himself to be manipulated is in for a very uncomfortable experience. The danger to the officer is rarely that of physical attack, rather he will feel greatly threatened psychologically. He may begin to believe that he is appearing foolish and damaged in his self-image (loss of face; receiving severe blows to his ego, etc.). Unless he retains his self-control, he may well commit a rash or illegal act which can easily result in disciplinary action or a civil suit naming him and his department as defendants. But the experienced professional officer never loses during these encounters because: He never presses or demands more than is absolutely necessary; Even though the law may empower him to do more; He always acts within the law and utilized it to accomplish its basic purpose, not just technical requirements which were designed to accomplish some other objective. His actions assure that his opponent becomes aware that: What the officer requires is within the law; The full extent of the available powers are never utilized without full reason; The officer never acts out of personal vengeance.

Professional Direction

ONLY ROOKIES TRY TO ENFORCE ALL THE LAWS ALL THE TIME, AND ONLY ROOKIES CONFINE THEIR ENFORCEMENT ACTIVITY ALMOST EXCLUSIVELY TO AN ARREST. The experienced professional officer has learned that enforcement of some laws is best accomplished by simply being present and visible. Other laws can be enforced by a warning or an educationally oriented conversion with actual or potential offenders. There are certain laws which do require that offenders be processed through the criminal justice system by either a summons or physical arrest. In most jurisdictions, with rare exceptions, no officer is in fact required to arrest for an offense except when ordered to do so by a magistrate, either by the judge in person or under his written order in the form of a warrant.

Criminal Law

A crime or an offense is an act or omission forbidden by law, prosecuted by the governmental officials of the jurisdiction, and punishable upon conviction. The statutes which define what acts or omissions are crimes or offenses must clearly state the kind of conduct which is prohibited or required and designate the punishment which is to be applied to those adjudged guilty.

Each statute which defines a crime is constructed of elements or criteria which the prosecution must prove before a defendant may be found guilty of the charge. The words used in statutes each have very special and particular meaning under law, and an officer must be careful to be aware of these legal terms because definitions in law sometimes differ from the meanings they convey when used in informal or daily conversation. For example, larceny or theft involves the *taking of the personal property of another*. Each of the underlined words is an element of the offense, and they are not the only elements. The "thief has not taken if he has not gained possession, it is not personal property if it is an attachment to a house, and it is not another's if the thief is a part owner or the property has been abandoned. Furthermore, even f he does commit all those acts, he has not committed theft unless he intended to steal. For example, the acts were committed under his reasonable belief that the property was his. Also, no matter how fervent was his intention to steal, there cannot be a conviction where the item "stolen" was not subject to ownership which is protected by law, for example an illegal lottery ticket.

Detentions

Police officers are empowered to make detentions and arrests under appropriate restrictions. A detention is a temporary restriction of one's liberty during which the detaining person is permitted to make a short investigation for the purpose of determining whether or not the person detained is subject to arrest for an offense. The authority and restrictions upon it which apply to this power of an officer are delineated by either court decisions or statutes, dependent upon the law which prevails within a particular jurisdiction. This type of detention is generally referred to as "stop and frisk." These three little words, however, have become the subject of thousands of pages of court decisions and statutes. This manual must cover the subject with just a few words, and readers should bear in mind that jurisdictions differ in what is permissible. Each officer should become well versed in the law on this subject as it is applied in his jurisdiction.

The stop and detention of a person is generally authorized when an officer has reasonable grounds for suspecting that the individual whom he intends to detain: has committed a crime, is committing a crime, is about to commit a crime.

Note that the facts on which the officer bases his stop and detention are less than those necessary for him to effect an arrest, and it is essential to his authority that the person to be detained must be suspected of criminal activity. An arrest requires that the officer has reasonable grounds for *believing* that the person has committed or is committing a crime, but a detention requires the officer to have reasonable grounds for *suspecting* involvement in criminal activity. Because the officer is possessed of information short of that required to make an arrest, he may not use deadly force to stop or detain the person.

An important factor in the laws dealing with detentions is that of the duration which will be permitted. In jurisdictions where the courts have delineated the law on this subject, case law permits officers to detain persons a reasonable time. The duration permitted is determined by the relative importance of permitting the officer time necessary to ascertain whether or not the person has committed a crime and the loss of freedom suffered by the person detained. Each case is decided on its own facts. Where statutes control, legislatures either permit a reasonable time, similar to court holdings, or specifically limit the duration, varying from ten minutes to two hours. Under both case law and statutes, however, an officer in every jurisdiction is required to release the person immediately after he has determined that the person has not committed a crime. Where the duration is limited to a specified time period, when the time limit has expired, the officer must either arrest the person for a crime or immediately release him, even though with more time to investigate the officer might have been able to develop sufficient information to effect an arrest.

Another critical difference among the various jurisdictions is the right of the officer to transport the person detained during the course of the investigation. In some jurisdictions the officer is not permitted to remove the person from the place at which the detention was initiated. In areas where it is permitted, the transportation must be conducted only when it is reasonably necessary for the purpose of investigating the possible criminal involvement of the person detained, and unless the investigation results in the person's arrest he should be returned to the place from which he was removed. The officer may ask any pertinent question of the person detained, for example his name, an explanation of what he is doing or where he is going, the ownership of any property in his possession, etc., but the officer must constantly remain aware that the person detained is under no obligation to answer any question. The detained individual may remain absolutely silent during the whole period of detention, is under no obligation to produce any identification or other property for the officer's inspection, and the office has no right to take *anything* from the person except a weapon.

Frisks

The frisk is a very limited search which may be conducted by an officer who has detained a person. It may be performed only when the officer: knows that the person has a weapon in his immediate possession; reasonably suspects that the person has a weapon in his immediate possession.

Note that the frisk is for weapons only, and that the officer must be able to state the facts which caused the development of his belief that the person possessed a weapon. The frisk: must be only for the purpose of locating the weapon; must be initially restricted to touching or grasping only the *outer* clothing of the individual; may be continued inside the outer clothing, pockets, etc. only after the officer has felt something which reasonably causes him to believe that a weapon is contained within.

If the officer finds a weapon, he may remove it from the person's possession. If the possession of the weapon on the part of the person constitutes a crime, the officer may arrest for that offense and retain the weapon as evidence. If the person is not arrested, the officer shall return the weapon at the end of the detention.

Arrests

An arrest is the deprivation of one's liberty by another for the purpose of initiating the arrested person's processing through the justice system, usually the criminal justice system. An arrest must be made in compliance with the restrictions which surround such an action. Otherwise, it is considered a false arrest and will cause the loss of the admissibility of any resulting evidence and possible loss of a conviction. The arresting officer may also possibly be subject to a suit for civil damages and be charged with a crime. An "arrest" which is made without the intention for processing the party into or through the justice system would be kidnapping within the statutes of most jurisdictions. Arrests can be made either under the authority of an arrest warrant or without a warrant, and the arresting person can be either a police officer or a person.

An arrest involves the following elements:

1. The arresting party "intends" to take the arrested person into custody. Although in most cases the arresting party's actual intention is to take the person into custody, and the best way to express this is by stating words such as, "You are under arrest for...," courts determine the intention from all the defend himself from false arrest liability by simply claiming that he had no intention to arrest.

2. The arresting party acts under the belief that he has legal authority. If the arresting party is correct in his belief the arrest is valid, but if he actually does not have the authority, it is an illegal arrest. Examples of lack of authority would be arrests made under a void or non-existent warrant, even though the officer had been informed that there was a warrant, and arresting for a misdemeanor not committed in his presence, if this is not permitted in his jurisdiction.

3. The arresting party gains custody and control of the arrested person. An arrest is not complete until the arrested person comes within the custody and control of the arresting party, and this state exists when either the person submits or his resistance is overcome. It is not necessary that the person be touched or that any force be applied if he understands that he is in the power of the arresting person and submits to control; that his liberty is restrained is sufficient. On the other hand, if the officer's words, "You are under arrest for..." are immediately followed by the suspect's running away, there has been no arrest. In fact, unless the flight includes some physical contact or the application of force between the suspect and the arresting party, the flight does not constitute resisting arrest.

An arrest warrant is an order of a court directing police officers to arrest and bring before the court the person named in the warrant. If it is practicable, an officer should obtain a warrant before making an arrest. The basic purpose served by the warrant process is to protect persons from unjustified arrests and prosecutions. The warrant is one of the manifestations of the checks and balances system in that a member of the judicial branch passes upon the legitimacy of actions intended by the executive branch. Given the same circumstances or facts known to an officer, if he arrests after obtaining a warrant, the courts will in all probability sustain the arrest, but if he arrests without one his action will be much more closely scrutinized for probable cause.

Following are common requirements for a valid arrest warrant:

1. Probable Cause: The magistrate issuing the warrant must make an impartial judgment on the basis of the evidence presented that probable cause exists that a crime has been committed by the person to be arrested. Probable cause is more than mere suspicion on the part of the officer requesting the warrant, but he is not required to present proof beyond a reasonable doubt of the person's guilt. Information supplied by informants may be used, even if their identity is not disclosed, but officers must be able to state facts which indicate the probable reliability of such information which they have not acquired through their own observation.

2. Affidavit supported by oath or affirmation. Some person must swear to his belief in the truth of the statements contained in the affidavit.

3. Person Particularly Described: The description must be such that the officer serving the warrant is supplied with information sufficient for him to believe with reasonable certainty that the person whom he is about to arrest is the person described. Ordinarily the warrant includes the name of the person, but sometimes this is not known. In such cases, a physical description, occupation or place of employment, residence address or other information may be utilized to particularly describe the person.

4. Nature of the Offense: Although the language need not describe the offense with the same detail as in an indictment or information, it must be sufficient to inform the person of the subject of the accusation.

5. Officers Designated: The warrant may direct an individual officer or a class of officers to arrest the person. For example, the warrant may be addressed to all police officers in the state.

6. Issued in the Name of the Jurisdiction: Warrants must be issued either in the name of the state under which the issuing magistrate's authority exists or in the name of the United States when issued by a federal official.

7. Signed by the Issuing Official: Only an official authorized by law may sign a warrant, and he must be a neutral and impartial person, a magistrate, or judicial officer.

Requirements to Be Followed in Serving a Warrant:

1. Person serving warrant must be named in it. Either the officer or person serving the warrant must be specifically named in the warrant or he must be within the class of persons designated.

2. Must Be Served Within the Jurisdiction: A warrant issued in one state may not be served in another unless the second state has authorized this service by statute. An officer in the second state may arrest if he has knowledge of the warrant's issuance; however, his knowledge constituting the reasonable grounds for his belief that a felony has been committed by the person.

3. Officer Make Known His Purpose: Unless the information will imperil the arrest or the person flees or resists before the officer can convey his intention, the officer must inform the person of his intention to arrest and the cause of it.

4. Show the Warrant or Inform Person It Exists: Under common law, the officer must possess the warrant and show it to the person if he demands it, but most modern codes have relaxed this requirement under the needs of today's society. However, the officer's belief in the existence of the warrant must be reasonable, and it shall be shown to the person as soon as practicable if he so requests.

Arrests can be made without a warrant by both officers and private persons. The authority of a police officer is more extensive, but not as much so as most people believe.

1. Both an officer and a private person can arrest for a felony committed in their presence and for a felony which has actually been committed but not in their presence.

2. An officer can arrest for a felony which he reasonably believes has been committed by the individual to be arrested, even though the crime has not been committed, but a private person may not. Stated in another way, the officer is protected if he makes a reasonable mistake, but the private person is not.

3. In all jurisdictions an officer can arrest for a misdemeanor which is committed in his presence, but in some jurisdictions a private person may not.

4. In some jurisdictions an officer may arrest for a misdemeanor not committed in his presence when he has reasonable cause to believe that it has been committed by the suspect, but a private person may not do so in any jurisdiction.

The Constitution, statutes, and court decisions refer to the necessity of the "reasonable cause" and "probable cause" which must exist before the authority to arrest arises. This degree of proof, evidence, or information to be possessed by the officer who intends an arrest must be more than good faith suspicion (enough to effect a detention for investigation), but it need not be proof beyond a reasonable doubt of the person's guilt. The reasonable cause is determined as of the time the arrest is effected. Evidence acquired after the arrest may not be utilized to validate a preceding arrest. In fact, if the arrest is not based on probable cause that evidence will be excluded no matter how condemning and conclusive it might have been in proving the defendant's guilt.

The standards by which an officer's reasonable cause to arrest is ascertained is determined individually for each case. That is, the information in his possession and its relationship to the development of probable cause in his mind (as opposed to a reasonable man test) in the light of his personal experience and the circumstances of the case before the court will all be considered by the court in arriving at its holding that there was or was not probable cause to arrest. Actions which do not attract the attention of untrained or inexperienced persons or officers may convince the experienced and trained officer that a particular offense is being committed. This experience may include not only the activity but also the person performing it. An officer who knows of the past criminal record of a suspect may consider that history along with other facts in developing reasonable cause, but the officer may not arrest on only the basis of one's previous criminal record.

The following are sources which can develop reasonable cause to arrest for the officer:

1. Complaints From Victims and Information From Witnesses: Statements and information received which indicate that a crime has been committed and which provide evidence by which the offender can be ascertained by developing reasonable cause to arrest. An officer must bear in mind that if the crime complained of is less than a felony no arrest will be valid unless a warrant is first issued, unless their jurisdiction is one in which officers are permitted to arrest for misdemeanors on reasonable cause. But if the jurisdiction is one in which private persons can arrest for misdemeanors, the victim or a witness can make the arrest and turn the prisoner over to the officer.

2. Information From an Informant: The reliability of the informant is an important factor. An officer should maintain records on the cases in which the particular informant's information has proven to be accurate, and whenever possible the officer should make further investigation to determine that the information is correct prior to making his arrest without a warrant.

3. Observation of the Officer: When the officer witnesses the actual commission of the crime, there is reasonable grounds to arrest without serious question. But when his observations lead him to a reasonable suspicion only, then he must first detain until his investigation leads to reasonable cause to arrest. When all the circumstances lead the officer to the reasonable belief that a felony has been committed, he may arrest under his reasonable belief in any jurisdiction, but for a misdemeanor only if his jurisdiction permits that type of arrest. An officer can always obtain a warrant and effect the arrest later for the misdemeanor.

4. Physical Evidence: Fingerprints, identification dropped at the scene of the crime, footprints leading from the scene of the crime to the place of apprehension, and other physical evidence closely tying the suspect to the crime would be sufficient to give rise to reasonable cause to arrest.

5. Information Received from the Officer's Department or From Another Agency: Information received over the police radio, at briefings, or from wanted circulars or lists may

form the basis for reasonable cause; however, persons initiating these messages must have reasonable cause for doing so.

Citation/Summons Process

The processing of offenders into the justice system is ordinarily begun when he is contacted by the police. At this point the person may be "physically" arrested and taken to jail or other place of detention to await his appearance before the court. Very few defendants want to spend time in jail, and the purpose of such incarceration is only to assure the appearance of the defendant before the magistrate. Originally, under our criminal law, incarceration to await court appearance was the only process utilized no matter what the degree of the offense. Beginning with the widespread use of the automobile and the numerous offenses committed by motorists, spurred by the growth of more liberal feelings toward offenders by both the general community and persons involved in the administration of justice, and because of the great savings in time and money which the method causes, written notification to an offender of the charge to be made and the time and place to appear before a magistrate has now become prevalent. Commonly called "a ticket," the citation or summons process is now not only used universally for traffic code offenses but has expanded to include many other types as well such as theft, assault, battery, a variety of regulatory statutes, and other misdemeanor offenses. Whenever possible or permitted, an officer should use this process.

The "ticket" procedure can proceed in three ways: an arrest followed by release, a detention followed by release, or the delivery of a notice of charges to be filed to the person charged. Although definitions differ somewhat, the citation process is that which involves an arrest by an officer followed by the offender's signing on the citation that he promises to appear in court at the time indicated, at which time he is given a copy of the citation and released from arrest. The defendant's signature and promise is his "bail." Should he fail to appear, he commits an offense which is separate from that of the original charge. The offender may refuse to sign the citation, but if he chooses to exert this right the officer is required to incarcerate him.

In jurisdictions in which the summons process is utilized, the offender is detained (not arrested) for a period necessary for the officer to determine the defendant's identity and write the summons, a copy is given to the person (he is not required to take it, and he is then released from detention. The suspect is not required to sign the summons, he commits no offense if he does not appear, and upon his non-appearance the court simply issues a warrant of arrest for the charge made.

The notice process involves leaving a written notice to be discovered by the person to be charged or otherwise delivering such notice, for example by mail. The vast majority of cases in which this process is used involves parking offenses, but it can also be utilized for many other offenses. Whether the person receives the notice or not, the charge is filed before the court, and if the defendant does not appear as directed in the notice, an arrest warrant will be issued by the court. Each officer must be aware of the law concerning these processes in his area because in many jurisdictions numerous offenses have been required by statutes and departmental regulations to be so handled. Therefore, an officer who incarcerates a person who is entitled under law or departmental regulation to be offered a citation or summons will be subject to prosecution, civil suit, and/or disciplinary action.

POLICE SCIENCE NOTES

FORCE, SEARCH, AND SEIZURE

Use of Force

The right to use force against another varies according to the reasonable and apparent necessity that it be applied. The most important factors considered in the determination of how much force may be used by an officer are the following:

1. Is the force used or contemplated essential, or could the actor reasonably foresee that less force would be sufficient?
2. Does the crime to be prevented or the arrest to be attempted involve a felony or misdemeanor?
3. Does the act or crime to be prevented by force endanger property rights or human life and limb, and to what extent?
4. What are the responsibilities under law between the actor and what or whom he is attempting to protect with force?
5. Do departmental regulations restrict officers to less force than that permitted by statutes and court decisions?

When necessary, a police officer is permitted to use force in the performance of his duty to accomplish the following objectives:

1. To preserve the peace, prevent commission of offenses, or prevent suicide or self-inflicted injury.
2. To make *lawful* arrests and searches, to overcome resistance to such arrests and searches, and to prevent escapes from custody.
3. To defend himself or another against unlawful evidence to his person or property.
4. To interrupt an intrusion on or interference with the lawful possession of property.

Lawful force is an aggressive act committed by a police officer in the performance of his duty when it is necessary to accomplish any of the objectives listed above. Deadly force is that which under the prevailing circumstances is capable of or intended to cause death or great bodily injury. Although lawful, or necessary, force is the minimum amount sufficient to achieve a legitimate objective, this does not mean that an officer is permitted to escalate the force he uses without limit until the police objective is accomplished. For example, it would be illegal and immoral for an office to use deadly force to prevent a person from unlawfully interfering with or even destroying anothers personal property such as an automobile, even if under the circumstances, shooting the person would be the only way the destruction could be stopped.

Deadly force may be used to prevent a felony which threatens the life or safety of a person. However, when the felony does not involve such danger, the tendency of the law among jurisdictions to prohibit such extreme measures is steadily growing. Even in those jurisdictions in which the statutes and court cases continue to permit deadly force to be used to prevent felonies in which life is not endangered police departments are prohibiting it through their policies and regulations.

Once a crime has been committed, the chief law enforcement interest is the apprehension of the offender. Although laws vary, deadly force may generally be used to effect the arrest of a dangerous criminal who is endangering or has threatened human life, but this amount of force may not be used on a thief no matter how much he stole. No jurisdiction punishes theft with the death penalty, so no officer should apply "capital punishment" to a thief.

In no jurisdiction is deadly force permitted to effect an arrest for a misdemeanor. If the subject resists, the officer may escalate the amount of his force until it becomes deadly, it this is necessary to protect himself from death or great bodily injury, and the officer is not required to retreat. However, the use of deadly force is not justified to apprehend a misdemeanant even though he is in flight and there is no other way to capture him.

The right of self-defense is based on the necessity of permitting a person who is attacked to take reasonable steps to prevent harm to himself. This right permits him to use any reasonable force to prevent threatened harm, offensive bodily contact, or confinement. Since it is a defense to a charge or accusation of use of force, the burden is on the actor to show the facts which caused him to use force and that it was reasonable.

The privilege to act to defend oneself arises not only when the danger is real but even when the danger does not in fact exist, providing that the belief in the presence and degree of anger is reasonable. For example, if after a long, high speed, wild and reckless attempt on the part of a motorist to escape an officer the offender stops, leaps from his car and whips his hand inside his jacket, it would be reasonable for the officer to believe that he was about to be fired upon. It would be lawful use of deadly force for the officer to draw and fire his sidearm at the offender even if, in fact, the motorist was unarmed and reaching for only his wallet and driver license. The belief that he is threatened, however, must be that which a reasonable man would have under the circumstances. The person defending himself is not required to restrain himself with outstanding bravery, but on the other hand the reasonable man standard does not permit an abject coward to attack when there is no reasonable ground for his belief that he is in danger.

If force is continued after at attacker is disarmed, defeated, helpless, or the danger has passed, it is unlawful. No matter how gross he provocation had been on the part of the original attacker, there is no right to continue the use of force for revenge or punishment.

No officer should possess or use any weapon or incapacitating device which is neither issued nor approved by his department, including the ammunition in his firearm. Naturally, issued or approved weapons which have been materially altered to increase the force which they may apply should also not be possessed or used.

Under normal circumstances only the methods or weapons listed below should be used to apply force. It is the officer's responsibility to first exhaust every reasonable means of employing lesser force before escalating to a more severe application of force. The following methods are listed in ascending order from the least severe to the most drastic:

1. Physical strength and skill
2. Approved noxious substance, mace, gas, etc.
3. Approved baton, sap, or blackjack
4. Approved sidearm or other firearm loaded with approved ammunition.

Weapons should never be brandished or displayed as a threat unless their use under the circumstances would be reasonable and lawful.

Only those security devices or measures issued or approved by the department should be used to restrain those in custody, and the devices and measures should be used reasonably and only for the purpose of preventing:

1. Escape
2. Destruction of evidence
3. Attack
4. Self-inflicted injury
5. Commission of an offense

An officer who, out of anger or for the purpose of inflicting punishment or pain, cinches handcuffs too tightly, places a person in a straight jacket, strips a prisoner naked, puts an offender into a padded cell, incarcerates an offender with others who may attack him, or continues security measures when they are no longer reasonably necessary is acting unlawfully and reprehensibly. It is the responsibility of the courts to punish, not the police.

The decision of an officer to use handcuffs or not is a difficult one. Opinions on this subject vary among experienced, professional officers. Where departmental regulations have been issued which state the circumstances under which handcuffs shall, may, or must not be utilized they should be followed. However, because of the difficulty involved in covering all the possible situations in a regulation, they have not been written for officers' guidance in many agencies. The officer must then utilize his professional discretion.

The officer who decides whether or not to use handcuffs on the basis of his answer to, "If I were this prisoner, would I realize or could I be lead to understand that handcuffs are reasonable and necessary?" will arrive at the appropriate conclusion. An officer who states that "I handcuff everybody I arrest," does not, it is to be hoped, really do so. It is obviously ridiculous to handcuff "little old ladies" and small children without exception. On the other hand, the officer who fails to restrain dangerous felons, persons in a state of rage, or others who can be reasonably expected to do any of the acts which security measures are designed to prevent certainly should be handcuffed.

An officer who fails to use his cuffs when it is appropriate endangers himself, his coworkers, the prisoner, and others. Persons who are restrained by security devices are helpless, and officers must remain constantly aware of the possibility that such prisoners may be injured or suffer needlessly if precautions are not utilized. Therefore, secured persons must not be left unattended unnecessarily or otherwise subjected to needless danger or discomfort. The variety of possible situations to be avoided are too numerous to mention, but two must be. Prisoners should never be handcuffed to a vehicle which is used to transport them. If the vehicle is involved in an accident, they cannot be removed from it if the officer is incapacitated or otherwise incapable of releasing them. It is appropriate to restrain handcuffed prisoners with safety belts because anyone can release the belts. However, if the person is handcuffed to the vehicle, only an officer can provide the key to the cuffs. Prisoners who indicate that they need to relieve themselves must be permitted to do so as soon as possible. The officer who refuses to permit his prisoner to use toilet facilities or to aid the nauseated person who must vomit is inflicting cruel and unusual punishment upon him.

Search and Seizure

The most important factor relating to the law of search and seizure, and what each officer should seriously consider before he begins any search for or collection of evidence is that WHENEVER POSSIBLE A SEARCH WARRANT SHOULD BE OBTAINED BEFORE SEARCHING FOR OR SEIZING EVIDENCE.

Both state and federal constitutions guarantee to everybody protection against unreasonable searches and seizures. This protection extends to their person, houses, papers, and other property. No search warrant may be issued without probable cause, supported by oath or affirmation, and every warrant must particularly describe the place to be searched and the persons or things to be seized.

The protection given by the Fourth Amendment arose from the unpleasant experiences suffered by colonial Americans when searches by English soldiers were conducted under the authority of "writs of assistance" or "general warrants." These writs and warrants were issued with little restraint, without probable cause, and empowered authorities to conduct searches virtually any place on the mere suspicion that goods subject to seizure might be discovered.

The words of the Fourth Amendment must be interpreted by the courts so that the meaning of the law can be applied to the fact situations of each case presented. Thousands of cases have defined "person," "houses," "probable cause," "search," and other words which appear in the Amendment.

Although persons subjected to unlawful searches and seizures have recourse to civil actions against officials who violate their rights, the most common procedure by which they protect themselves is through the application of the exclusionary evidence rule. The exclusionary rule is simply that evidence obtained by unreasonable searches and seizures will not be admitted upon trial, usually upon objection raised by the defendant at a pre-trial "suppression hearing." The rule is not provided for in the Constitution, rather it was developed by the courts as their solution to the means by which the provision of the Amendment would be enforced, not adopt it. Today, however, it is universally applied in both federal and state courts because of the holding of the Supreme Court of the United States in the case of Mapp v. Ohio in 1961. The purpose to be fulfilled by the rule is that officers will be deterred from illegally searching for or seizing evidence when they know that it cannot be used against the defendant to prove his guilt.

Search Warrants

A search warrant is an order written in the name of the State, signed by a judicial officer in the proper exercise of his authority, directing a sheriff, constable, or other officer to search a specified place for evidence, stolen property or other "fruits" of a crime, or contraband, and to bring the articles enumerated before the court if they are discovered.

The following are criteria or requirements which must be met before a valid search warrant may be issued:

1. **Probable Cause**

   If the facts in the affidavit are sufficient to lead a reasonable and prudent man to believe that a crime has been committed and that the articles described can be found at the place specified, then issuance of a search warrant is justified. Information received by an officer from an undisclosed informant may be used as the basis for a search warrant, but the applicant for the warrant must be able to give the judicial officer substantial reasons to support the probable validity of the information which has been provided. The underlying circumstances upon which the applicant bases his belief must be specified by him. It is not sufficient to merely state, even with fervor, the police officer's belief. The facts of which he is aware which led to the development of that belief must also be stated.

2. **Oath of Affirmation**

   If this requirement is not fulfilled, the evidence obtained will not be admitted. The presumption that the magistrate had sworn the applicant is rebuttable by the defendant, and if no oath was administered the warrant is invalid and the evidence will be lost (excluded).

3. **Particular Description of Place and Things**

   Whatever the wording to describe the place to be searched, the objective to be served is that the officers who are commanded to conduct the search will not, if they follow the description included in the warrant, search the wrong premises and disturb the rights of the innocent. If the warrant does not identify the property to be seized, it will not justify any seizure of that property. Contraband such as prohibited arms, explosive devices, and gambling equipment will ordinarily not be required to be as specifically described as stolen goods, since contraband is sizeable by any officer lawfully observing it. When warrants are obtained for contraband, the best description possible under the circumstances should always be attempted.

4. **Issuing Official**

   The purpose served by requiring warrants is to assure that the innocent will not be disturbed by uncontrolled and unreasonable actions of officials of the executive branch of government. Therefore, the impartial and objective consideration by the judiciary of the probable cause and the reasonableness of the contemplated action is interposed as a restraint. Attempts to bypass this objective, even to accomplish other well-founded purposes such as the efficient issuance of warrants, have generally been found unconstitutional by the courts.

5. **Property Subject to Seizure**

Under early law, only stolen property could be seized under a search warrant. However, types of articles subject to seizure have been greatly expanded. Limitations still exist in some states such as requiring that only stolen or embezzled property (fruits of the crime), articles used to commit the crime (instrumentalities), or articles which are prohibited or controlled by statutes (contraband) may be seized. Such restrictions prevent officers from taking objects which are important as evidence, such as shoes worn by a suspect which could be compared with footprints found at the scene, but which fail to meet the definition of statutory restrictions. The United States Supreme Court in *Warden v. Hoyden* held in 1967, that statutes which permitted search warrants to issue for "mere evidence" are constitutional. It is up to those states which still follow the old rule to change their statutes or court decisions to permit seizure of evidence, but they are not required to do so.

Only those items specified in the warrant may be seized. If other property is seized, it must be under authority other than that provided by the warrant.

6. **Execution Only By Those Ordered**

A search warrant may only be executed by those commanded by it to act, but the person designated may be specifically by either name or class (peace officers, for example). The person designated may be assisted by others, however.

7. **Time Limit**

A search warrant must be executed within a reasonable time or it will fail to meet constitutional requirements. The amount of time which is reasonable varies, of course, according to the circumstances of each case. Most jurisdictions have by statute limited the time in which a search warrant may be executed, and the permissible period varies from a number of hours to more than a week. Some jurisdictions require special judicial authorization for warrants to be served at night

8. **Prior Notice, Demand, and Forcible Entry**

If the local law allows and the warrant is for the seizure of items which can be destroyed quickly or if officers are aware of facts which reasonably lead them to believe notice to occupants would lead to danger of attack, entry may usually be effected without notice. Otherwise they are first required to notify persons within the premises of their identity and right to enter and make a demand that they be permitted to enter. Reasonable and necessary force may be used to effect entry when officers must act quickly to avoid evidence destruction or attack, or if they are denied entry after notice has been given and their demand had been refused. Force may also be used to enter unoccupied premises or when the denial is passive, for example, when occupants remain silent and do not open the door.

Warrantless Searches and Seizures

Three factors have influenced and caused the development of those laws under which warrantless searches are permitted. They are permitted and lawful:

1. By consent
2. When necessity or emergency require immediate action
3. Where no right to protection exists

Consent Searches

A general principle of law is that one can waive any right or privilege to which he is entitled. However, because rights and privileges have arisen from previously experienced problems, court observe very carefully the evidence presented in support of contentions that a defendant consented to a search.

Consent must be voluntary, the prosecution has the burden of proving consent clearly, and some sort of positive action by the person waiving must be shown. For example, unless the person positively states his consent or makes some clearly understood gesture, the consent will not be held to be voluntary.

The search cannot extend beyond that granted by the terms of the consent in either area or time. That is, consent to search a room will not permit other rooms or the whole house to be searched, and the person may stop the search at any time simply by revoking his consent.

The person consenting must have the capacity to do so. A person who has the right to possess premises or things may give consent, but others may not. For example, the occupant of a hotel room may consent to its search but not the management, a parent can consent to a search of a minor child's room but not that of an adult child if the room is exclusively that child's, although permission to search areas used in common by the family is valid; a minor child's consent is unlikely to be held valid, but an adult child can consent to a search of at least jointly used areas; a spouse can consent if the premises are occupied by both spouses; and a person caring for the personal property of another may permit search of it.

Immediate Action Required

The most prevalent situations under which this exception is granted are searches made incident to a lawful arrest. Necessity is the motivating factor in permitting these searches. The two purposes served are to protect the arresting officer from attack and to prevent the person from access to things which would facilitate his escape, and to assure that evidence will not be destroyed by the defendant.

Should any of the following criteria not be met, the evidence discovered will be excluded:

1. The arrest must be lawful.
2. The search must be made for the purposes listed above (protection, security, evidence).
   An arrest for an unlicensed vehicle, to be followed by a citation, may not be the basis for a search for drugs as there is no relationship between the offense and the purpose of the search.
3. The arrest must not be a sham or subterfuge made only to initiate a search not based on reasonable cause.

An arrest warrant sworn out by officers (who merely suspect a burglary by the subject) charging the defendant with spitting on the sidewalk for the purpose of gaining entrance to his residence when they execute it, evidence of the burglary would be excluded.

Both the area searched and the time during which the search will be permitted are limited. Officers may make a reasonable search of areas within the person's reach or the distance through which he might be able to quickly leap in order to obtain a weapon for attack or evidence to destroy. Searching for evidence during an arrest beyond this area is no longer permitted without a search warrant. The search must be made contemporaneously with the arrest. After the subject has been removed from the scene and/or confined in jail, the necessity of immediate action no longer prevails, and the officer must obtain a search warrant to search the area of the arrest. An arrested person may be immediately fully searched, as opposed to a mere pat-down for weapons, incident to an arrest for which he is actually being taken into custody, or the search may be delayed until booking.

Once in jail, an arrestee or his property room effects may be researched without a warrant where the searches are not unreasonably made, i.e., harassment searches.

The right of officers to search a car beyond the reach of the subject being arrested, for example in the closed trunk or even the locked glove compartment,, would have to be based on grounds other than the arrest itself, i.e., on probable cause to search those areas, on consent, or "plain sight," or on a valid inventory.

When probable cause exists and the evidence is contained within a moving (or about to be moved) vehicle, officers may search. There is a significant difference in the necessity for immediate action between searches of buildings and searches of vehicles which may speedily be moved out of the jurisdiction before a search warrant can be obtained. An occupied car on a highway is movable, and the persons within it are alerted to the presence of officers. The evidence may never again be located if courts were to require officers to obtain a warrant to search under these circumstances. To conduct a warrantless search of a "moving" vehicle, the officer should have that amount of information which would cause a court to readily issue a search warrant if there were time to procure one. The officer may make the search without first arresting the person. The search will be upheld under the vehicle exception if the essential requirements of probable cause are shown to have existed prior to the search.

Where No Right to Protection Exists

Seizures of evidence without a search is not a violation of the Fourth Amendment when officers are lawfully present and the article seized is seen by them. Courts do not require officers to leave obvious evidence to be destroyed, but officers must not be trespassers at the time the evidence is observed. Furthermore, if an officer is a trespasser when he does see evidence, he cannot then procure a search warrant on the basis of the information he acquired as a trespasser.

The protection offered by constitutional provisions are to protect persons against the acts of government officers, not private parties. Therefore, if a private person obtains evidence through unlawful entrance or burglary, the evidence may be used against the criminal defendant. Of course, if an officer initiated the private person's action or participated in it, the evidence would be excluded. Searches and seizures are unlawful when they reasonably intrude into areas where the person can reasonably expect privacy, but not outside those areas. Open fields, public streets, and other places of similar description are outside the restrictions of the Fourth Amendment.

Inventories of vehicles which come into the hand of the police through impounding procedures are permitted. The inventory made of the vehicle is for the purpose of making an inventory of its contents to protect the owner rather than a search for evidence of an offense. The officer's intrusion is only justifiable if it is a good faith attempt to protect the property in the car. In effect, the evidence is discovered "accidentally" while the officer is doing what he has a right to do and where he has legitimate cause to be.

POLICE SCIENCE NOTES
PATROL

INTRODUCTION

Patrol is commonly referred to as the "backbone" of police activity. It serves as the foundation upon which all other police functions rest. It is the fundamental operation which contributes greatly to the successful curtailment of criminal activities. Police patrol is also a basic factor in providing the public with the type of police service that it has a right to expect.

The word "patrol" comes from the French "Pattrouiller" meaning "to go through puddles." This is an excellent description of the task because good patrolling means going through puddles, through garbage-filled alleys, and up rickety back stairs in all kinds of weather and at all times of day or night.

While patrol is neither glamorous nor exciting at all times, it can be interesting and rewarding for the individual officer. It gives the officer an opportunity to observe a wide variety of people and supplies insight into their problems. By being alert and understanding, he can analyze his beat area and render effective public service.

The continuous patrol of an area, whether on foot or in a vehicle, makes or breaks a law enforcement agency. Nothing contributes more to police efficiency and the belief of the community in its security and protection by its police than the manner in which patrol duty is performed. Patrol is truly the police department's first line of defense against crime.

PURPOSES OF PATROL

The general purposes of patrol might be stated as follows:

1. The protection of life and property.
2. The preservation of the peace.
3. The prevention of crime.
4. The detection and apprehension of criminals.
5. The regulation of conduct (noncriminal).
6. The performance of required services such as giving aid and information.

These are the tangible, definite things for which police patrols are designed, but on the other side, there are certain intangible things that are very important, but cannot be reduced to exact actions. The policeman on the street is more than just an officer on patrol; he is the police department in the eyes of many of the people and indeed, he represents all of government to a large portion of the public. This factor indicates the leadership role which the policeman is called upon to play in time of civil defense emergency or natural disaster. So, it is doubly important that he know and execute his task well. In no area of his work is the policeman required to exercise tact, good judgment, and leadership as often as while he is patrolling.

TYPES OF PATROL

There are three general classifications of police patrol which are pertinent here. They are foot patrol, vehicular patrol, and plainclothes patrol.

Every patrolman is a foot patrolman at one time or another. There are two types of foot patrol, moving and fixed. An officer on moving patrol is assigned to a designated route or beat to cover. This route is generally in an area where there is a concentration of police hazards. An officer on a fixed post has primary assignment at one location, such as traffic direction at a specific intersection. Much of the work to be done falls within this category.

Vehicular patrol includes the performance of many of the same functions that are required of the foot patrolman. The basic difference can be found among these factors:

1. The use of some mode of transportation, i.e., bicycle, motorcycle, horse, boat, aircraft, or most often, automobile.

2. The ability to cover a larger geographic area.

3. The existence of constant radio contact in most instances.

While vehicular patrol may also involve moving or fixed assignments, fixed vehicular patrol is normally only employed when communications contact is imperative.

Plainclothes patrol may be foot or vehicular, moving or fixed. It is normally used only to handle special problems such as the control of criminal activities in areas of high-crime frequency or surveillance of specific persons or locations.

POLICE PATROL TECHNIQUES

Efficiency in patrol can be attained only through considerable experience. There are, however, a number of tested techniques that the auxiliary policeman should know and practice.

While patrolling his assigned area, the patrolman should "be systematically unsystematic." The officer should frequently backtrack and take an unexpected route whether in a vehicle or on foot. He should maneuver so as to observe the people and locations on his beat without in turn being observed. This can be done properly only if the dead ends, construction work and any other factor which might cause delay. The patrolman must also have knowledge of the legitimate activities and crime potentialities of his area.

The location of stores, service stations, other houses of business and their hours, is vital knowledge to the beat officer. Knowledge of these things will enable him to more readily recognize some unusual activity that may possess criminal implications. This knowledge is also useful to the officer because it will enable him to intelligently direct persons asking for information. It is, thus, essential for the officer to know the area which he is patrolling.

Observation is also an important tool for the patrolman. It includes the utilization of all of his senses in ascertaining just what is occurring in his area of responsibility. Observation is a result of intelligent curiosity, and it can and should be developed. The officer should carefully take in all aspects of life around him as he walks his beat. When anything out of the ordinary takes place, he should evaluate it and take the steps that are necessary. The required evaluation is of the utmost importance and it will necessitate years of experience before the officer's faculties are developed to a peak of efficiency. The officer should, however, constantly practice his observational technique because only through such constant exercise can he expect to achieve effectiveness.

Particular care should be taken when observing individuals. Personal description is critical to the patrolman's task. Every officer should learn the procedure employed by his department for identifying suspects or wanted persons.

SOME THINGS TO WATCH FOR WHILE ON PATROL

While patrolling an area, an officer should be careful to observe the following things:

1. Doors and windows in buildings those are not secure. If any are found, the officer should search the premises, secure the premises with any means at hand, and notify the owner through appropriate channels.

2. Conditions conducive to crime such as: improperly secured buildings, partitions between stores, things of value left unattended, and window displays and counter displays of unusual value.

3. Suspicious persons or known criminals. The officer should also observe suspicious behavior such as: loitering around banks, warehouses, shipping rooms, dock terminals, schools, hotels, stores, etc.; door-to-door peddling, begging, delivery services strange to the area; and persons with no apparent destination or purpose.

4. Business places. These should be scrutinized carefully on each tour. The officer should ascertain the following information concerning each of them: location of safes and cash registers; location and type of night lights, and alarm systems; habits of the staff; exits; means of locking doors, windows, gratings, skylights, basements, etc.

5. Vehicles. The patrolling officer will find them important to his work. They will often be the thing most likely observable in connection with criminal activities. Many excellent arrests and much fine police work have resulted from observation of vehicles. Traffic enforcement, of course, requires close observation of vehicles, but the officer on patrol must not confine his interests only to traffic violations.

6. Signs of disorder, excitement or unusual activity such as: large groups of people, hysteria at the scene of a fire or other disaster, drunk or quarrelsome persons, persons running away from or toward some incident or location, or people avoiding the police or watching police activity.

7. Conditions which are hazardous or require actions such as the repair of sidewalks, streets, street lights, and various fire hazards. In some instances, the officer should take remedial action himself. In other cases, he should report the condition through the proper channels.

INFORMATION AND ASSISTANCE

Besides his various activities in the area of crime control, the police officer to called upon by the public for information and assistance. It is important that he handle these request with dispatch and accuracy. This is especially true in time of emergency and disaster. The correct performance of such actions also tends to result in greater public cooperativeness.

AT CRISIS LOCATIONS

Patrol duties in fallout and crisis locations, while involving the same basic principles discussed above, will also be concerned with situations peculiar to crowded and unfamiliar conditions. The following list of such situations is suggestive, not exhaustive.

1. Hazardous conditions, such as insufficient ventilation, fire hazards, etc.

2. Violations of regulations, such as smoking at unauthorized times or places, unnecessary noise while others are trying to sleep, horseplay, scuffling, etc.

3. Evidences of poor morale or emotional disturbances.

4. In general, all situations about which the authorities should be kept informed, such as evidence of boredom, illness, behavior problems of small children, etc.

CONCLUSION

Patrol is the backbone of police service. Without constant vigilance on the part of the basic patrol unit, the patrolman, the police cannot hope to accomplish their objectives under normal or emergency conditions. It is, then, critical that the individual officer extend himself as far as possible in the performance of this indispensable police activity.

www.ingramcontent.com/pod-product-compliance
Lightning Source LLC
Chambersburg PA
CBHW080324020526
44117CB00035B/2643